SŌTŌ ZEN

*The Very Reverend Keidō Chisan Kohō Zenji, Abbot of Sōji-ji
and Archbishop of the Kantō Plains, author of this book.*

SŌTŌ ZEN

An Introduction to the Thought of the

Serene Reflection Meditation

School of Buddhism

by

THE VERY REVEREND

KEIDŌ CHISAN KOHŌ ZENJI

Edited by

REV. JISHŌ PERRY, M.O.B.C.

SHASTA ABBEY PRESS

MOUNT SHASTA, CALIFORNIA

First Edition—2000
Second Printing—2001

© 2000 Rev. Jishō Perry

Shasta Abbey Press
3724 Summit Drive
Mt. Shasta, California
96067-9102

Printed in the United States of America.

Published by Sōji-ji Temple, Tsurumi-machi, Tsurumi-ku,
Yokohama, Japan, 1960.
Edited and reprinted with permission.

ISBN: 0-930066-09-X

LIBRARY OF CONGRESS CARD CATALOG NUMBER: 99-071360

The TransIndic Transliterator font used to print this work is available from Linguist's Software, Inc.,
PO Box 580, Edmonds, WA 98020-0580 USA   tel (206) 775-1130.

THIS BOOK IS DEDICATED TO THE
BUDDHIST SANGHA.

The Sangha is one of the Three Treasures of Buddhism. The first is the Buddha, which can be understood as the historical Buddha, Shakyamuni, and the Unborn, Undying Buddha Nature which was realized by the Buddha at the time of his Enlightenment. The second Treasure is the Dharma, which can be understood as the teachings that have flowed from the realization of the Unborn. The third is the Sangha Treasure. In its narrowest sense it is the Buddhist priesthood, and in its wider sense it is all those beings, lay and monastic, who are sincerely training themselves to realize the same Truth as was realized by the Buddha. The initial harmonization of body and mind was realized by Shakyamuni Buddha, who exclaimed "I was, am and will be enlightened simultaneously with the Universe," and therefore the Sangha can be seen as the harmony that exists throughout the universe as a result of the training and realization or actualization of the Truth when beings learn to work in harmony within themselves and with all living things. The Sangha Treasure also represents Harmony in its widest sense, the harmony of all living things. Being human we sometimes focus so much on the differences that we forget the underlying harmony that unites and flows through all living things. Homage to the Sangha.

Every morning in Buddhist temples throughout the world, monks put on their kesas and say a small verse. It is a reminder that every day a monk needs to focus on his or her spiritual purpose and renew the vows taken at ordination. In the Order of Buddhist Contemplatives we say that verse in this manner: "How great and wondrous are the clothes of enlightenment, formless and embracing every treasure, I wish to unfold the Buddha's teaching that I may help all living things."

ACKNOWLEDGEMENTS

I wish to acknowledge and express profound gratitude to the following for helping with the production of this book: The Very Reverend Keidō Chisan Kohō Zenji for writing this book and inviting Rev. Jiyu-Kennett to come and study with him; my late teacher, Rev. Master Jiyu-Kennett, former Abbess of Shasta Abbey and founder of the Order of Buddhist Contemplatives; Rev. Master Daizui MacPhillamy, the current Head of the Order; Rev. Master Ekō Little, Abbot of Shasta Abbey; Rev. Shikō Rom, Head of Shasta Abbey Press; Rev. Mokugen Kublicki who provided the beautiful portrait of Kohō Zenji used on the back cover; Rev. Meidō Tuttle; Rev. Kōten Benson; Rev. Meiten McGuire; Rev. Oswin Hollenbeck; Rev. Zenshō Roberson; Rev. Chūshin Passmore; Rev. Koryū Noguchi and the Japanese monks who gave permission for the publication of this book; Professor William Powell and Professor Keiko E. Mochizuki and many others who helped with this book and encouraged me to work on and complete this manuscript. All photographs except the scroll on the half-title page are courtesy of Shasta Abbey.

CONTENTS

INTRODUCTION

In 1960 when this book was originally published, the author, the Very Reverend Keidō Chisan Kohō Zenji was the Abbot of Sōji-ji, one of the two main temples of the Sōtō Zen Sect in Japan. Many Westerners had visited the temple after World War II; this book was written to introduce them to Sōtō Zen, or the Serene Reflection Meditation School of Buddhism. During a tour of the United States and Europe, Kohō Zenji called on the then President Eisenhower and asked for and received permission to spread the teachings of Sōtō Zen in America. Although to the politically sophisticated American this may seem either naïve or unnecessary, it is the traditional Buddhist approach to respect the laws and the political leader of a country and to ask permission before giving the Buddhist teaching. On that same tour when in England he met a woman, Miss Peggy T.N. Kennett, who was to become his disciple and eventually bring his Transmission of the Sōtō teachings to America and Europe. Kohō Zenji invited her to come to Japan and study with him at Sōji-ji. This was a remarkable and unusual event to invite a person who was a woman and not a native of Japan to officially study at one of the two main seminaries and monasteries of the Sōtō School. In Japan Kohō Zenji had championed the cause of education for women, and he did not stop with schools for girls and nurses. He was willing to risk the censure of those who clung to the cultural norms of his country in order to follow the teachings of Buddhism. "One of the greatest teachings of Buddhism is its insistence upon the complete equality of the sexes."*

On her way to Japan Miss Kennett was ordained by Rev. Seck Kim Seng in the Chinese Rinzai tradition in Malaysia. Upon her arrival in Japan she was received by Kohō Zenji as his personal disciple. He gave her the name Hōun Jiyū, which means Compassionate Friend within the Dharma Cloud. Rev. Jiyu-Kennett studied with Kohō Zenji in Sōji-ji until his death in 1967 (the story of her training is published by Shasta Abbey Press in *The Wild, White Goose*, Vols. I and II) and then came to America in 1969, where in 1970 she founded Shasta Abbey in Kohō Zenji's name. Out of gratitude for the great gift of the teaching, one would never found a monastery or temple in one's own name, but in the name of one's teacher from whom the great gift of the Dharma was received. Shasta Abbey is a training seminary and monastery and has become the headquarters of the Order of Buddhist Contemplatives. The Order also includes another seminary and monastery, Throssel

---

* Great Master Dōgen, *Shushōgi (What is Truly Meant by Training and Enlightenment)* in *Zen is Eternal Life*, 4th ed., by Rōshi P.T.N.H. Jiyu-Kennett (Mt. Shasta, California: Shasta Abbey Press, 1999), p. 99.

Hole Buddhist Abbey in Northumberland, England, as well as priories in the U.K., Canada and the U.S.A. Throughout the Order the teachings of Kohō Zenji are being followed today.

In originally publishing this book it was Kohō Zenji's wish that people in the West could study Buddhism in the context of their own language and culture. It is an easy and common mistake to get the culture and language confused with the religion and adopt the cultural forms without understanding the religious practice that underlies them. Rev. Master Jiyu-Kennett, M.O.B.C., has manifested her teacher's wish in making the Buddhist teaching available in English throughout the English-speaking world. Out of gratitude to Kohō Zenji and Rev. Master Jiyu-Kennett this book is being republished in the hope that others may wish to find in Sōtō Zen, or the Serene Reflection Meditation tradition, the cure for suffering that the Buddha so compassionately offered to the world.

The text has been edited for spiritual clarity, and some of the terminology revised to reflect current usage; unfortunately the original Japanese was not available for comparison. Many of the original quotes from Great Master Dōgen, who brought this tradition from China to Japan in the 13th Century, have been replaced by Rev. Jiyu-Kennett's translations from her book, *Zen is Eternal Life*. Although the translations were not available in 1960 when *Sōtō Zen* was originally printed, they are being used in this edition to better convey the meaning of

Great Master Dōgen's understanding. While Rev. Jiyu-Kennett was in Sōji-ji, Kohō Zenji was instrumental in helping her translate Great Master Dōgen for the spiritual accuracy of his teaching and not for literal precision of the words. This same spirit was used in editing this text.

It is republished with the kind permission of Sōji-ji and Kohō Zenji's disciples and grand-disciples in Japan to whom we wrote. Although some of the information reflects the situation in 1960 and is no longer current, the great bulk of the teaching and information contained herein is timeless.

We pray for peace in all the world;
We pray that evil may be overcome by good;
We pray for harmony in the Sangha,
and for the cessation of all disaster.

Editor,
REV. JISHŌ PERRY, M.O.B.C.
Santa Barbara, California
April, 1997

United States President Dwight D. Eisenhower meeting the Very Reverend Keidō Chisan Kohō Zenji at a reception in the White House.

The Very Reverend Keidō Chisan Kohō Zenji receiving Rev. Jiyu-Kennett as his personal disciple, taken at Sōji-ji, Yokohama, Japan, 1962.

FOREWORD

Zen Buddhism, a religion which originated in India, has shown a rich development as a result of its contact with the intellectual culture of India, the practical culture of China and the artistic culture of Japan. Although it is a religion, its influence has been extended to fields outside pure religion. Buddhist meditation is the basis for Oriental culture. The simple but profound characteristics of this meditation can be seen everywhere and have played an important role in helping human beings realize their innate adequacy. Buddhism has been introduced to Europe and America, attracting the attention of many intellectuals. Conspicuous progress has been made by the materialistic civilization of the West, but this has unfortunately resulted in the enslavement of modern man by machinery. Men are never free from unrest and uneasiness. Machines are nothing but a means and are not the goal. Only when man is the master of himself can he live a true, meaningful life. Japan has imported advanced science from Europe and America. Science, beyond doubt, is one of the essential elements of present civilization. Although we cannot afford to ignore science, we also cannot allow science to go its own way without regard for the welfare of mankind. Science should be guided and directed by a religion based upon morality.

Zen Buddhism is a religion in which man can realize the Truth through just-sitting meditation [in Japanese this is called *shikan taza* or *zazen*]. The Truth means the direct experience of oneness with the Eternal.* We may also call it Buddha Nature. Zen Buddhism is the religion in which Buddha Nature is realized through practicing meditation and applying the meditation to all aspects of our daily life: training. The author of this book is a follower of Zen Buddhism in general and a follower of Sōtō Zen in particular. Sōtō Zen is one of the five meditation schools of Buddhism in China. It combines practice and understanding, stress being placed upon thorough practice. Thorough practice means practice in which man never neglects the details of daily life but leads the fullest existence without the slightest trace of deception. Sōtō Zen in Japan shows a considerable development over the Sōtō Zen in China. If one believes that man is already enlightened from birth, one must regard our daily activities as post-enlightenment exercises. In Japanese this is termed *honshōmyōshū*, or "original enlightenment and marvelous training." These exercises are, moreover, acts of gratitude to Shakyamuni Buddha. In Japanese this is called *gyōjihō-on*, or "the expression of our gratitude through religious training."

---

* The Buddha referred to the Buddha Nature as the "Unborn, Undying, Unchanging, Uncreated" in the *Udana Scripture*; Keizan calls It "the Lord of the House." The original translation of *Sōtō Zen* refers to It as "true human nature." Sometimes it is referred to as "the Absolute."

This is one of the characteristics of the Sōtō Zen Church of Japan, which was founded by Great Master Dōgen and further enlarged by Great Master Keizan.

It is often said that "Rinzai is for a general and Sōtō for a farmer," and indeed Sōtō has found its way into the hearts of the common people. Since it is a religion into which ordinary people can easily be initiated, it is only natural that it has developed into a large religious school. The Sōtō Zen Church has established an inseparable contact with the people of Japan and revealed a true way of living for us to follow. It is by no means asceticism. The Buddhist ideal has always been the middle way, free from extremes. Buddhist meditation teaches the way to true life, independent of both asceticism and pleasure, discarding the contradicting views of existence and non-existence. The aims of Sōtō Zen are thorough training, harmonization of body and mind and transcending the extremes of dualistic thinking. It is said that in the West, Zen generally means Rinzai Zen. However, I hope that people in the West will realize that in addition to Rinzai Zen, there is another great tradition in Zen, that of Sōtō Zen, or the Serene Reflection Meditation tradition, which is at once both philosophical and practical, and will, I believe, appeal to the people of the West. This is the reason why I have written this book.

CHISAN KOHŌ

SŌTŌ ZEN

1.

The Coming World Culture

The word "culture" is etymologically derived from "culti-vation," i.e., turning the wilderness into something ideal. It is, so to speak, the idealization of nature. Culture differs from civilization in that it contains many spiritual elements. The English historian Arnold Toynbee sets up various classifications for culture. Generally speaking, culture can be divided into two groups: Occidental and Oriental. Developments in transportation facilities have greatly reduced the size of the world. The different countries of the world have come to resemble each other to the extent that we sometimes have to stop and think how and where we are to draw the line between Oriental and Occidental culture. Nevertheless, the East and the West each have basically different cultural characteristics.

The characteristic feature of Western culture can be found in its development of modern science. The source of this culture must be sought in ancient Greece. The Greeks endeavored to the utmost to explain the "form" of things. This spirit later became the source from which science was produced. However, it was necessary to pass through a long process of development until modern science could evolve. Up until the eighteenth century, science was little more than pious learning. Only after the nineteenth century did science become an independent branch of study. Essentially, science is that field of scholarship which carries out experiments, observes, classifies and collects various objects to give a rational explanation of them. The aim of science is to systematize knowledge, removing all inconsistencies and rejecting all arbitrary interpretations. As the result of science, mankind has received great benefits and enjoys unlimited advantages.

Oriental civilization, on the other hand, is moral and religious in contrast to the scientific character of Western civilization. The main religions of the world originated in the Orient and its adjacent areas. Occidental culture is directed outward, Oriental culture, inward. The former tried to cultivate the wilds of nature while the latter tried to refine the untamed mind through mental cultivation. Indwelling life is the subject matter of Oriental culture. Life is the source for building new things in the midst of unending motion. Religion, philosophy and, in the broad sense, morality explain our existence and take up the question of understanding birth and death: the purpose of life. In particular, religion stems from the pressing demands of our indwelling life and sets as its goal our living within our Real Selves. Religion is the force by which man lives. When man loses sight of his spiritual purpose, life becomes suffering and man falls into despair. The chief characteristic of Oriental culture lies in its religion which is rich in spirituality and philosophy. Its fountainhead is Indian culture in which there is both the idea of infinity and the inherent immaculacy or emptiness of all form.

Neither scientific Western culture nor religious Eastern culture can, by itself, be considered complete. In Oriental culture science is necessary; in Occidental culture, religion. Here is the key with which we can bring about the synthesis of the Oriental and Occidental cultures. Both cultures, while preserving their special characteristics, must possess the magnanimity to continue to search for what is good and to remove from its midst what is not. The future world culture must have as its foundation a religious spirit which embraces science. Science is built upon humanistic thinking which in its essence means respecting, educating and liberating humanity, thus including at once both thought and action. The object of science, in accordance with the demands of humanism, is the happiness of mankind.

Likewise, religion has the responsibility of bringing about the salvation of mankind by finding the cause and the cure of suffering. It is the force which sustains human existence and is derived from the deepest recesses in man. Thomas Carlyle compared religion to the eternal stars in the sky: as the darkness of night covers the earth, the brilliance of the stars grows ever brighter in the sky.

Although we must respect science to the utmost, we cannot overlook the fact that human life requires something more than science alone. But so long as science is based partly on supposition, its uniformity can be only partial and cannot extend to the whole of life. It remains abstract and not concrete. Science cannot survey broadly the meaning of the world and human life nor explain the capabilities of man or the position in which he finds himself. Therefore, we contend that it is not omnipotent. We must fully understand the objectives of science and integrate them into the experience of daily life. This can only be done by something outside of science: the religious spirit. Science together with religion will show men how they can find the cause and cure for suffering and free themselves from the attachments that perpetuate the cycle of birth and death. Religion, however, must include and embrace science. If religion places too much stress on miracles and becomes unscientific, it will not be able to fulfill its mission.

Toynbee's new world history is written from a viewpoint that attempts to reveal a universality in which there is a lofty rationalism trusting in science, a progressive humanism emphasizing the respect for and emancipation of mankind, and a discarding of narrow provincialism. The religion of the future cannot overlook these points: 1) freedom of the spirit, 2) respect for reason, 3) tolerance toward other religions, 4) respect for all beings. Freedom essentially is the right to follow one's own conscience without being subject to any outside pressure. To be able to choose our own religion is also a matter of freedom. It is impermissible to compel anyone to adopt specific religious beliefs. This is the meaning of freedom of religion. It is only natural that we should want to choose a religion on a high cultural level which is suited to our own individuality. The religion of the future must respect reason. Religion by its very nature is more suited to emotion than to reason. The world of religion belongs to a realm above philosophy and science, which depend solely upon reason. Nevertheless, we do not say that religion is opposed to science. A religion which opposes science and is only suited for inner devotion is superstition. The religion of the future must not fall into this error. If a religion of the future is to go hand in hand with other ideologies, it is necessary for it to have a theoretical foundation. The struggle between science and religion in the West which continued for many centuries victimized a great number of scientists. Buddhism, however, does not shun the absorption of scientific knowledge. It feels rather that science plays an important role in revealing the course that religion should follow. Dr. Hideki Yukawa, winner of the Nobel Prize, emphasized the need for wisdom to guide modern science.

The religion of the future also must be more tolerant toward other faiths. As faith must be suited to individual needs, it is unreasonable to insist upon the uniformity of different faiths. It is natural that there should be many different religions. Human existence is essentially conflicting. On the one hand, man is weak and cruel; on the other, strong and compassionate.

The former causes him to reflect deeply on his sinfulness and to seek the Absolute outside himself to whom he can give himself in order to attain salvation. The latter enables man to seek the Absolute within himself and to try to live in harmony with his True Self as reflected in the light of the Absolute within him. Religion may be classified broadly into these two types. Everyone is free to search for either a transcendental God or to awaken the indwelling God. For this reason it is utterly impermissible to force a religious faith on anyone. It is necessary to be tolerant toward all religions. The prejudiced attitude which breeds such bigoted sentiments as "Only my religion is true" deserves sharp criticism. Toleration will appear when religions approach each other and seek to deepen mutual understanding. It is, after all, just a question of common sense and etiquette, as is readily observable among civilized people.

We have already said that the religion of the future must be based upon respect for all beings, which means respect for and the education and emancipation of humanity. There are three ways of expressing this in Japanese. Their nuances differ, yet these three words agree on the one point that they all show respect for mankind. Religion must also respect, educate and deliver humanity from affliction. If religion will adhere to these ideals, it can be firmly established and can be confident of realizing its objectives. The religious spirit which is capable of embracing science will form the basis upon which a new world culture will be built.

Western culture which developed scientifically may be called a culture that emphasizes existence (Ger. *das Sein*; J. *yū*). However, the mere suggestion of existence implies also non-existence (J. *mu*), for the concept of existence could not arise unless it were contrasted with non-existence. Oriental culture is based on this idea of mu,* non-existence, immaculacy, purity. (Although *mu* is variously translated as non-existence, immaculacy, Buddha Mind, etc., it will not henceforth be translated for it has no exact equivalent in English.) *Mu* is the principle of selflessness which enables us to penetrate to the very core of the finite and, by embracing and transcending (J. *hōetsu*) it, to bring about a change from knowing only the limitations of self to directly experiencing the immaculacy and purity of That which

---

* The concept of *mu* is frequently translated as emptiness and means more accurately emptiness of self or selflessness. Some people frequently feel fear at the idea of emptiness, imagining some spiritual black hole from which one can never be extricated. Rev. Jiyu-Kennett described It as "the fullest emptiness you'll ever know." She frequently used words like purity, immaculacy and "the Eternal" to describe It in a way that would not mislead or frighten people. Buddhism does not use the idea of God precisely because it frequently implies a separation between man and God. The concept of *mu,* however, cannot be separated from any "thing." The Buddha used the concept of the "Unborn, Uncreated, Unchanging" to point at what is experienced in enlightenment. Sometimes it is more accurate to describe the Absolute by what It is **not** than by what It is. It is difficult for those who do not know It directly to understand that a negation can be something brighter and more positive than any "thing" previously experienced.

is selfless. It is precisely this ideal which underlies Oriental religion, philosophy, morality, art, etc. However, although mu forms the basis of Oriental civilization in general, its manifestations in India, China and Japan are quite different from each other owing to differences in geographical conditions and national characteristics. Because Indian culture, like that of the Greeks, is a product of an Aryan people, its tendencies are both intellectual and philosophical. Chinese culture is neither religious like the Indian nor philosophical like that of the Greeks, and is distinguished by its preoccupation with the practical. Japanese culture, on the contrary, is neither intellectual nor practical, but essentially emotional. Its sensitivity to beauty (J. *mono-no-aware*) is discernible by the way in which the Japanese bring man and nature into relationship with each other and eliminate the distinction between such opposites as "inside" and "outside." A culture heavily charged with emotion (J. *jō no bunka*), which goes directly to the True Nature of things, gave the Japanese people such concepts as *wabi* and *sabi* (highly developed aesthetic taste which should be "felt" rather than intellectually defined). The essence of these concepts lies in simplicity and profundity. Buddhism has permeated every Oriental country and, in the process, has revealed its own special characteristics after having combined with the intellectual culture of India, the practical culture of China and the emotional culture of Japan.

2.

The Basic Thought of Buddhism

Does a religious spirit which can embrace science exist anywhere in the world? The [late] President of the London Buddhist Society, Christmas Humphreys, says, "Buddhism is a system of thought, a religion, a form of mental science, and a way of life. It is practical and all embracing. For over two thousand years Buddhism satisfied the spiritual needs of one-third of humanity and is very suitable for Westerners because it has no dogma. It satisfies reason and emotion equally, and while teaching us to follow our own convictions, it stresses toleration for other peoples' ideas. It nourishes science, religion, philosophy, psychology, ethics and art and holds that man is the creator of his present life and the architect of his destiny."

Buddhism is the teaching of the Buddha, the teaching of how to become a Buddha. It is a religion which enlightens us to the fact that we are already enlightened. "Buddha" means in Sanskrit "the Enlightened One" and is applied to a person who has attained to Perfect Enlightenment and is capable of using this enlightenment to awaken in others the seeds of enlightenment. The Buddha is held to be a man who awakened enlightenment in himself and who also awakened it in others. His personality is characterized by Perfect Compassion and Perfect Wisdom; because of Wisdom, he achieves enlightenment for himself; because of Compassion, he endeavors to enlighten others. The main object of religion is to enable us to understand ourselves. Reflection upon the realities of life is the fastest and shortest way to find ourselves. Socrates says, "Know thyself," and Dōgen teaches, "When one studies Buddhism, one studies oneself; when one studies oneself, one forgets oneself; when one forgets oneself one is enlightened by everything and this very enlightenment breaks the bonds of clinging to both body and mind not only for oneself but for all beings as well." [*Zen is Eternal Life*, 1999, p. 206.] Self-reflection on reality is the starting point of philosophy and is the basic condition of religion. We are standing at a point which intersects two lines: one of time and one of place. Our point on the time line is "now" and on the place line, "here." This is reality. Reality means we are born here, work here, and die here. It is, so to speak, the actual place of our life. Buddhism describes the vertical, i.e., time, aspect of reality with the oft-quoted phrase, "All things are impermanent," which means that all phenomena are in a continuous state of flux. According to this law, all matter, which we may be tempted to regard from a common sense point of view as having a permanent, fixed existence, is essentially in a state of motion, continuously undergoing change and radiating energy. Many centuries ago Buddhism taught principles which agree with conclusions that science arrived at only yesterday.

However, Buddhism is a religion, not a finite science. But it is a religion which does not contradict science, but rather assimilates it. The law that all things are impermanent teaches us that we cannot spend one moment without experiencing some activity and demands that we live in Truth. Each moment is a sacred segment of time which can never be repeated. This life comes only once. There can be no other experience for us aside from the one in our present life. Therefore, it is essential that we arouse in our hearts a fervent vow to realize enlightenment. The last words of the Buddha to us at his Parinirvana [death] were: "All things are impermanent. Strive hard, freeing yourself from all corruption." The Zen School says, "Both life and death are a serious matter. The law of impermanence is in continuous operation. You must strive hard to save yourself from the flames of passion that burn from within. The perfection of each second, the grasping of each moment, must be the result of a correct understanding of the law of impermanence."

Buddhism uses the term *innen shōsho*: literally, coming into existence because of direct and indirect causes (Skt. *hetu-pratyaya*), and the term *engi*: literally, arising from cause (Skt. *pratītya-samutpāda*), to indicate the horizontal, i.e., space, aspect of reality. *Engi* shows that all things are mutually dependent upon each other and that nothing can exist independently. One is held by the other and in its turn holds the other. Each thing plays its part in forming the chain of totality. Einstein's theory of relativity denied the absoluteness of time, space and motion and stressed the interrelationship of all things. The relationship between the individual and society is also subject to this law. From the universe down to the individual, nothing exists which is not dependent upon this principle. Buddhism does not recognize fixed, permanent existence but only one of relationships. Buddhism arrived at this conclusion, which is in agreement with science, by the intellectual-intuitional method. We see a good example of this in the thought of Whitehead.

Looking at this from a religious point of view, we must conclude that the fact that we are able to live peacefully is due to outside support and to social blessings which we enjoy. Therefore it is the natural duty of man to express his gratitude for these benefits. Not to know gratitude is to be on the level of an animal. If we examine the nucleus of a thing, we shall observe that everything directly or indirectly runs into and is dependent upon it and that nothing within the thing is independent of the nucleus. The nucleus contains and unifies all the parts. Now let us assume that we are the nucleus under discussion. We are dependent upon many factors which when combined enable us to live. We can only live peacefully so long as this is true. We must concretely express our gratitude for the great favors of the Buddha and Ancestors who made clear the way for us to understand ourselves. Shinran Shonin declared, "We must recompense the Tathagata (Buddha) for his great compassion no matter how great the sacrifice. We must recompense our teacher for the knowledge he has bestowed upon us no matter how great the effort." An understanding of *engi* (the law that all things arise from cause) will awaken within us a deep sense of gratitude toward the world and will lead us to the practice of *rita-gyō*, literally, "benefiting others," for it will enable us to see to what extent we enjoy the benefits of others.

The point mentioned above where time and space intersect is where our Real Self is. In the West our self is affirmed as it is. There is no denying its naturalness or sense of instinct. However, in the Orient we do not accept ourselves in our present form. We idealize the natural and try to purify our instincts. Buddhism teaches that there is no ego or unchanging soul. As nothing has a permanent existence, there is no sense in clinging to things. Common sense seems to indicate that matter really exists. However, this is misleading. The tying together and functioning of our sense faculties lead us to believe that there is a soul. However, there is no soul apart from the body. To negate ourselves and grasp the real nature of things is nothing other than the scientific spirit. M. Planck, the founder of the quantum theory, said, "Scholarship moves forward because of the selfless cooperation of many scholars who devote themselves exclusively to the search for truth without any self-seeking interest." Buddhism considers self-centered attachment to desire and ignorance as to the True Nature of things to be the source of suffering. Shakyamuni Buddha respected the laws of human life and the universe, recognized the True Nature of things and, rejecting all arbitrary metaphysical speculation, stressed the need to question our assumptions. The wisdom found in the *Hannya Kyō* (Skt. *Prajñā Sūtras)* is not in conflict with scientific knowledge. Accordingly, here in the East we do not see the struggle between science and religion that occurred in the West, resulting in the persecution of scientists.

The law of impermanence declares that nothing has a real (in the sense of unchanging) existence and that therefore we must avoid all words and actions which tend to make us cling to things. From a religious viewpoint all actions arising from the desire to receive personal gain are a source of suffering. Our True Self will appear when we negate our lustful self (i.e., our self considered from the view point of egoistic gain). This may be regarded as the turning point of self or as a fundamental reform in our life. All religions seek this self-denial. It is a subjective awakening to the fact that we have no eternal self (Skt. *ātman*). Only when we rid ourselves of the false self can we find our True Self. The gospel of St. Paul says, "I live; not I, but Christ." The Chinese Buddhist monk Sōjō (C. Seng-chao, 384–414) writes, "The true saint neither has a self nor has not a self." If we can discard a thing as small as our self, then we can experience a thing as large as the universe.

We can arrive at selflessness only by robust faith. Desire for personal gain is nothing more than the dictates of our lustful self. Selflessness, on the other hand, does away with the distinction between oneself and others and achieves a fundamental unity rich in all-embracing compassion which makes us vow to accept all beings, rejecting none. This vow is truly a manifestation of the heart of Buddha. At the same time that the Buddha transcends us, he is embracing us.

The laws Buddhism teaches are all organically related to each other. Each of the three fundamental ideas that "all things are impermanent," "all things arise from causation," and "all things are without self, (Skt. *ātman*)," contains the other two ideas within itself. Therefore, although Buddhism teaches these three ideas, we can say that in reality there is but one basic idea expressed in three different ways. When we deeply experience these laws with our mind as well as body, then we shall achieve the quiet of nirvana. This quiet is describable as an absolutely peaceful state of mind which is arrived at through enlightenment which conquers ignorance and extinguishes the flames of lust, thereby developing within us a compassionate personality abounding in wisdom. We are enlightened as to how to live in Truth ourselves and how to lead others to live in Truth. It may be said that compassion and wisdom are the twin pillars of Truth. Wisdom means to know the True Nature of the universe and human life; compassion means to embrace all, rejecting none. The three laws given above are called collectively the three signs of Buddhism, for they represent the most essential characteristics of Buddhism. The law of causation has a particularly close relation to the other two laws which teach impermanence and selflessness. The former law functions because all things have the latter two characteristics. To know this is to have achieved the peace of nirvana. In Mahāyāna Buddhism we combine these three signs and say that they are but the One Sign which reveals the True Nature of all things. When we view the nature of things with the eyes of enlightenment, we see that all things are manifestations of Truth. In order to arrive at such enlightenment it is absolutely essential to have grasped thoroughly the idea of *kū* (Skt. *śūnyatā*), i.e., that nothing has a fixed, unchanging existence.

The law that all things are impermanent, based on the doctrines of causation and no-soul, ultimately developed into the concept of kū expounded in the Scriptures of Great Wisdom, *Hannya Kyō* (Skt. *Prajñā Sūtras*). Buddhism rejects all attachments, because it regards life as being filled with an everflowing vitality constantly undergoing change. The law of causation, aided by the laws of impermanence and no-soul, was gradually deepened and led to the doctrine of phenomenal identity of the *Kegon Kyō* (Skt. *Avatamsaka Sūtra*). Phenomenal identity is the name given to the idea that all phenomena have a deep, inseparable interrelation. Everything is related in both time and space to everything else, forming an inseparable whole, yet functioning freely. The law of the non-existence of the soul, supported by the laws of causation and impermanence, led to the development of the idea of the Buddha Nature (Skt. *Buddhatā*) found in the *Nehan Gyō* (Skt. *Parinirvāna Sūtra*). The Buddha Nature is the essence of the Buddha. It is That which makes him Buddha. According to the *Nehan Gyō*, all beings possess this nature and are thereby assured of realizing enlightenment.

Although differences do exist among the various schools of Mahāyāna Buddhism as to emphasis, we may generally say that the three laws given above form a basis for Mahāyāna. But Zen is not content to acknowledge these laws conceptually. It insists upon experiencing them concretely as well.

3.

The Origin and Development of Zen

Zen, like Buddhism itself, is a product of India. However, its antiquity is far greater than that of Buddhism. Its origin is connected with the custom of Indian philosophers who sought an escape from the heat by dwelling in forests. Here they spent their time in meditation and observance of religious ceremonies. This practice of sitting in a prescribed posture beneath a large tree to meditate was regarded as a pleasant religious exercise. This ultimately developed into zazen, just-sitting meditation or the serene reflection practice of Zen Buddhism. Zen is the Japanese pronunciation of the Chinese word *ch'an*, which in turn is a phonetic transcription of the Prakrit *jhāna*, suffering the loss of its final vowel. The Sanskrit equivalent of *jhāna* is *dhyāna* which means "meditation, thought, reflection, (especially) profound and abstract religious meditation." The Upanishads, which deal with Brahminic philosophy, may be considered a product of this type of meditation in forests. The number of Upanishads is very great. The first occurrence of the word *dhyāna* is in the Chandogya Upanishad which is one of the oldest of the Upanishads. In early Sanskrit translations into

Chinese the word was rendered "thought and practice." In the later translations the term "quiet reflection" was chosen. The former meant concentrating the mind on one object, thinking about it thoroughly and then carrying it out into practice. The latter term had reference to the practice of putting the heart at rest in order to see things more clearly. This word for meditation has also been translated as the Japanese term *jō*, i.e., fixed, stable. This has reference to fixing the mind on one object in order to free it from distractions. The form of *dhyāna* which flourished before the rise of Buddhism lacked completeness in both method and form.

Buddhism gave new meaning to *dhyāna,* deepened its contents and defined its objectives clearly. We might also say that this meditation strengthened the foundations of Buddhism as a religion. It is with this in mind that Oldenberg said, "Zen (meditation) is to Buddhism what prayer is to other religions." Hermann Beckh wrote, "The only way to understand correctly the difference between Buddhism and other religions is by a comparison between Zen meditation in Buddhism and prayer in other religions." Buddhism owes its success as a great world religion to the fact that Zen meditation forms its practical basis. Indeed, the enlightenment of the Buddha was realized through the practice of Zen meditation. There is nothing unnatural then in the fact that Buddhism has its roots in Zen. Although the form of Zazen practiced by the Buddha was the same as the earlier non-Buddhist meditation, its contents were quite different in that the serene reflection meditation of the Buddha was based on the premise of the identity between body and mind and did not recognize the existence of an eternal soul. It was an indispensable religious exercise aimed at realizing the perfection of human character in this life.

Zen has always served as the foundation for many virtues esteemed by later generations. Kuei-Feng Tsung-mi (J. Keihō Sumitsu), a learned priest of the T'ang Dynasty, in the preface to his *Explanations as to the Origins of Zen* distinguishes five kinds of Zen: 1. Non-Buddhist Zen (J. *Gedō Zen*); 2. Popular Zen (J. *Bompu Zen*); 3. Hinayāna Zen (J. *Shōjō Zen*); 4. Mahāyāna Zen (J. *Daijō Zen*); 5. Zen of the Highest Vehicle, Serene Reflection Meditation (J. *Saijōjō Zen*).

Non-Buddhist Zen, rejecting this world, has as its object rebirth in heaven. It is found in the Yoga School, one of the six schools of Indian philosophy, and was also the type of meditation practiced by Ālāra Kālāma and Udraka Rāmaputra, two teachers under whom Siddhartha studied after becoming a monk. They considered Zen meditation itself as their final goal, hoping to be born after death in one of the heavens corresponding to the stage of Zen meditation they had reached during their life. They regarded the mind and the body as two separate entities, believed in the existence of an eternal soul and sought supernatural powers.

Popular Zen may be considered an amateurish kind of Zen practiced by people who accept Buddhism and, despising the afflictions of this world, try to realize the joy of liberation. Since these people aim at escaping from the world of illusion to find happiness, they have not progressed beyond the stage of the judgmental or discriminatory mind. Accordingly, it is difficult for them to enjoy truly peaceful serene reflection meditation, which is found when one goes beyond the opposites.

Hinayāna Zen is the meditation practiced by people who have arrived at the stage of selflessness, transcending all traces of judgmental or discriminatory thinking. However, although its followers have subjectively realized the non-existence of the soul in man, they have not yet come to understand that matter too is devoid of a permanent, fixed, unchanging existence. Therefore we may consider this kind of meditation one-sided. Hinayāna Zen utilizes very complex categories. It has enriched later generations by its concept of meditation.

Mahāyāna Zen is that form of meditation which has achieved an understanding of the Truth arising from the denial of both a permanent unchanging self or soul in man and the permanency of things. This idea, *kū* in Japanese (Skt. *śūnyatā*), denies the validity of all concepts which hold that things have a fixed existence. Through *kū* we can see the real nature of things. The Scriptures of Mahāyāna are nothing but an attempt to reveal the contents of the Buddha's Great Experience through writing. If we wish to grasp the basic spirit of Buddhism and to live according to that spirit, the only path for us to follow is that of Zen. The fact that the Mahāyāna Scriptures were preached by the Buddha either on the occasion of his entering serene reflection meditation or after he emerged from meditation must always be kept in mind. The *Hannya Kyō* (Skt. *Prajñāpāramitā Sūtra*) was preached in the *Tojio Zammai*; the *Hokke Kyō* (Skt. *Saddharma Pundarīka Sūtra*) was preached in the *Muryō Gisho Zammai* (Skt. *Anantanirdesa Pratisthāna Samādhi*); the *Kegon Kyō* (Skt. *Avatamsaka Sūtra*) was preached in the *Kaiin Zammai*; the *Nehan Gyō* (Skt. *Parinirvana Sūtra*) was preached in the *Fudō Zammai*. The meditation practiced by the Bodhisattvas in China before the establishment of the Zen School as well as the meditation of the Sanron School, Tendai School, Kegon School, etc., is included under this heading of Mahāyāna Zen.

The Zen of the Highest Vehicle is found in the Serene Reflection Meditation Tradition transmitted by Daruma Daishi (Skt. Bodhidharma, C. Ta-mo Ta-shih) which teaches that man's nature is originally pure and untainted, that he possesses inherent wisdom from the time of his birth and that his heart is Buddhahood itself.

Daruma was the third son of the king of Kōshi, a state in southern India. Deploring the decline of true Buddhism, he left his homeland on a distant voyage to China, arriving somewhere

to the south of Canton about 470 C.E. He later went to Lo-yang
(J. Rakuyō), the capital, and settled in the Shao-lin (J. Shōrin)
Temple located on Mt. Sung (J. Sū) where he practiced unin-
terrupted meditation. This period in his life is generally called
"the nine years of wall gazing" (J. *mempeki kunen*). Daruma's
teachings are collectively known as "The Two Entrances and
Four Deeds" (J. *Ninyū Shigyō*). "The Two Entrances" are:
1) the entrance into Buddhism through reason or understanding
(J. *rinyū*) and 2) the entrance into Buddhism through deeds
(J. *gyōnyū*). Entrance through reason is the term applied to the
realization that we have the same heart as that of the Buddha.
We may attain this knowledge through the guidance of a good
teacher. The entrance into Buddhism through deeds is the name
applied to the realization in practice that all beings have the
Buddha Heart. This realization is nothing other than what we
experience in serene reflection meditation and in our daily life.
The essence of Daruma's teaching is the enlightenment and
practice which arise from the knowledge of the existence of the
Buddha Heart. The Buddha Heart is revealed in the wisdom of
enlightenment and the practice of serene reflection meditation.
Daruma transmitted the Truth to Hui-k'o (J. Eka), who in turn
passed it on to Seng-ts'an (J. Sōsan). From Daruma to Seng-
ts'an the Transmission was direct from master to a single
disciple. They practiced the twelve *dhutas* (J. *zuda-gyō*, ascetic
exercises), lived contentedly in poverty with no fixed residence

and made it a rule not to spend more than one night in any one place. Accordingly, it was not possible for these first three Ancestors to exert much influence on society in general.

However, the Fourth Ancestor, Tao-hsin (J. Dōshin), and the Fifth Ancestor, Hung-jen (J. Kōnin), settled on Mt. Shuang-feng (J. Sōhō) in Huang-mei District (J. Obai) in Chi-chou (J. Kishū, present-day Hupei Province) for a period of sixty years and surrounded themselves with more than five hundred disciples. It was under such conditions that Zen was transformed into a Chinese religion. When many people live together, it is not possible for them to devote themselves entirely to formal meditation and other religious matters. In order to live they must pay due regard to daily chores such as sweeping, cooking, farming, etc. In order for such work to assume the same degree of importance as is attached to the formal meditation, it becomes necessary to grasp thoroughly the meaning of Buddha Nature and Buddha Heart. Thus Zen was gradually deepened spiritually and made to meet the needs of ordinary living. Zen henceforth was not to be relegated to the meditation hall of a temple, but would come forth to play an active part in all aspects of society.

The Zen School teaches that we should not be dominated by the Scriptures, but rather we should use them for our own needs, that we should not adhere to a literal interpretation of Scriptures, but apply their teachings to our daily living. This

School thus made regulations to cover collective living as found in the large monasteries and thereby sought to supplement the lack of Mahāyāna temple regulations concerning religious observances and etiquette. These regulations are known by the name of *Ch'ing-kuei* (J. *shingi*). The Ch'ing-kuei may be regarded as a combination of the Indian *vinaya* (that part of the Scripture which contains the Precepts) and the Chinese *li* (J. *rei*, rules of etiquette and ceremony).

The Fifth Ancestor, Hung-jen, had about seven hundred disciples among whom the two most famous were Shen-hsiu (J. Jinshū, 606–706) and Hui-neng (J. Daikan Enō, 638–714). Shen-hsiu, who founded the Northern School of Zen, had studied both Confucianism and the doctrines of Lao-tzu and Chuang-tzu (J. Rōshi, Sōji) in his youth. He later was converted to Buddhism and read extensively in the Buddhist Scriptures and followed the Buddhist Precepts. At the age of fifty, he became a disciple of the Fifth Ancestor and studied under him for six years, until finally it was said, "The Law (Transmission of the Dharma) of the Eastern Mountain (Hung-jen's residence) will be found in Shen-hsiu." He was renowned for his deep learning and great virtue and was called the Master of the Law of the twin capitals, Lo-yang and Ch'ang-an (J. Chōan). Two emperors (Chung-tsung and Jui-tsung) and one empress (Wu-hou) studied under him. Hui-neng, the founder of the Southern School of Zen, came from a poverty-stricken family. The story of how he supported his aged mother by selling firewood is famous in Buddhist history. Later in his life he entered the monastery of the Fifth Ancestor and there worked in the granary for eight months. He was finally chosen Ancestor by Hung-jen and thereupon withdrew to Ta-yu-ling (J. Daiyu-rei) for a period of sixteen years. The year after he formally accepted the Precepts of Buddhism (formal monastic ordination), he entered the Pao-lin (J. Hōrin) Temple. Later, on the invitation of the magistrate of Shao-chou (J. Shōshū), he moved to the Ta-fan (J. Daibon) Temple. It was here that he preached the main portions of the Sūtra of the Sixth Ancestor (C. *Liu-tsu T'an-ching*, J. *Rokuso Dangyō*).

The Sixth Ancestor then moved to Mt. Ts'ao-ch'i (J. Sōkei) and resided there for thirty-eight years propagating Buddhism in Shao-chou and Kuang-chou (J. Shōshū, Koshū). When Hui-neng had become sixty-eight years of age, Emperor Chung-tsung, acting on the suggestion of Lao-an (J. Rōan) and Shen-hsiu, invited him to lecture at the palace, but Hui-neng, claiming illness, refused.

Shen-hsiu believed that all beings possessed the Buddha Nature. However, he regarded delusions (Skt. *kleśa*) as something real, teaching that they must be removed gradually through strenuous efforts. His school of Zen is therefore termed "gradual enlightenment through real practice." The Zen of Hui-neng, on the other hand, holds that the Buddha Heart, which all beings naturally possess, is an indivisible union of the wisdom of enlightenment and meditation found in religious observances. Illusion and affliction are originally non-existent. Therefore, religious observances cannot be regarded as merely a means to rid oneself of illusion, but must be thought of as a practice of enlightenment, or enlightenment in practice. In Zen we call this "sudden enlightenment—wonderful practice" (J. *tongomyōshu*).

Among the fifty students of Hui-neng, the two most prominent are Nan-yüeh Huai-Jang (J. Nangaku Ejō, 677–744) and Ch'ing-yuan Hsing-su (J. Seigen Gyōshi, died 740). The leading disciple of Nan-yüeh was Ma-tzu Tao-i (J. Baso Dōitsu, 707–786) and that of Ch'ing-yuan was Shih-t'ou Hsi-ch'ien (J. Sekitō Kisen, 700–790). Ma-tzu was nicknamed Ta-chi (J. Taijaku), Lord of Kangsi, and Shih-t'ou, Lord of Hunan. The Lin-chi (J. Rinzai) and the Wei-yang (J. Igyō) Schools are derived from the line of Ma-tzu, whereas the Ts'ao-Tung (J. Sōtō), Yun-men (J. Ummon) and Fa-yen (J. Hōgen) Schools emerged from the line of Shih-t'ou. Zen teaching theoretically holds to the doctrine that one's own heart is Buddha (J. *sokushin zebutsu*) and that the path to enlightenment is to be found in one's own heart. However, owing to the individuality and differing personalities of various Zen masters, it is only natural that their methods of teaching should differ vastly, thus inevitably giving rise to many schools. Among the eighty-four disciples of Ma-tzu, the most prominent is perhaps Po-chang Huai-hai (J. Hyakujō Ekai, 749–814). He built for the first time a Zen monastery centering around a meditation hall, and, breaking away from the traditional Buddhist *vinaya*, he established a new set of temple regulations called *Ch'ing-kuei*, previously mentioned above. Among his thirty disciples, the two most influential were Huang-po Hsi-yün (J. Ōbaku Kiun, died 856) and Wei-shan Ling-yu (J. Isan Reiyū, 771–853). The disciple of Huang-po was the famous Lin-chi I-hsuan (J. Rinzai Gigen, died 867), who lived in the Lin-chi Temple to the southeast of Chen-chou-ch'eng (J. Chinshujō). He revealed a new style in Zen and was endowed with great vitality. His line flourished and came to exercise great influence on the entire Buddhist world. Wei-shan Ling-yu settled on Mt. Ta-wei (J. Daii) where his disciples over a period of forty-two years numbered more than a thousand. Yang-shan Hui-chi (J.Gyōzan Ejaku 807–883), a disciple of Wei-shan Ling-yu, served his master for fourteen or fifteen years, then moved to Mt. Ta-yang (J. Daiyō) in Yun-chou (J. Enshū) where he carried on the tradition of his teacher. The meditation practice of Wei-shan and his pupil Yang-shan formed the basis for the Wei-yang School. This was the first of the Five Schools of Zen Buddhism in China to grow extinct.

One of the disciples of Shih-t'ou was Yüeh-shan Wei-yen (J. Yakusan Igen), whose disciple was Yun-yen T'an-ch'eng

(J. Ungan Donjō). The disciple of Yun-yen was Tung-shan Liang-chieh (J. Tōzan Ryōkai, 807–869) who early in his career lived on Mt. Hsin-feng (J. Shimpo) where he propagated Zen meditation. Later he moved to Tung-shan in Yun-chou (J. Enshū) where he gathered around himself several hundred disciples. His disciple Ts'ao-shan Pen-chi (J. Sōzan Honjaku, 807–883) taught Buddhism first on Mt. Chi-shui (J. Kissui) in Fu-chou (J. Fushū). Later he moved to Mt. Ts'ao (J. Sō), hence his name Ts'ao-shan Pen-chi. His pupils were exceedingly numerous, always filling the lecture hall. The Ts'ao-Tung School (J. Sōtō) derives its name from this Ts'ao-shan and his master, Tung-shan. However, the line of Ts'ao-Tung (J. Sōtō) coming from another of Tung-shan's disciples, Yun-chu Tao-ying (J. Ungo Dōyō, died 902), flourished most.

The Yun-men School (J. Ummon) was founded by Yun-men Wen-yen (J. Ummon Bun'en, 864–949), who is the fifth disciple in direct line from Shih-t'ou. The names of the intervening four disciples are T'ien-huang Tao-wu (J. Tennō Dōgō), Lung-t'an Ch'ung-hsin (J. Ryūtan Sūshin), Te-shan Hsuan-chien (J. Tokusan Senkan) and Hsueh-feng I-ts'un (J. Seppō Gison). Wen-yen visited all of the famous monasteries after he had been chosen successor of I-ts'un, his master, and revealed his own distinctive style of teaching. Later he converted the governor of Kuang-chou, Liu Kung (J. Ryū Kyo), and had many occasions to lecture on Buddhist meditation before the court. The Yun-men School together with the Lin-chi School were the most popular in China. The Fa-yen School (J. Hōgen) was derived from the teaching style of Ch'ing-liang Wen-i (J. Shoryo Bun'eki), who is third in the line descending from Hsueh-feng, the intervening two being Hsuan-sha Shih-pei (J. Gensha Shibi) and Lo-han Kuei-ch'en (J. Rakan Keichin). Following Wen-i's enlightenment under his master, Kuei-ch'en, he moved to Lin-ch'uan-chou (J. Rinsen-shū). Subsequently he was invited by the magistrate of the area to settle in the Ch'ung-shou Temple (J. Chuji) where he gathered about him no less than a thousand disciples. Later he moved to the Pao-en Ch'an Temple (J. Hōon Zen) in Chin-ling (J. Kinryō) at the invitation of Lieh-tsu (J. Resso). Still later he became the chief abbot of the Ch'ing-liang Temple to which many Buddhist priests were drawn by his lectures. His school of Buddhism, known as the Fa-yen School, is a blend of Sōtō and Hua-yen (J. Kegon) thought. Unfortunately, few of the priests of this School were able to exert a far-reaching influence.

In summary, Lin-chi is characterized by a sternness of spirit and complete freedom; Wei-yang, by a sudden identity of minds between master and disciple engaged in a serious exchange of questions and answers; Ts'ao-Tung (J. Sōtō), by an absolute unity between practice and understanding and the wholehearted use of ceremonial as devotional service; Yun-men, by the use of unique phrases to get rid of delusions;

and Fa-yen, by a practical use of the sayings of the masters to dispel immediately all the illusions which disturb the Buddhist student.

The Huang-lung (J. Oryō) School was founded by Hui-nan (J. Enan), who was a disciple of Tz'u-ming Ch'u-yuan (J. Jimyo Soen), who was a sixth generation disciple of Lin-chi in a direct line. Fang-hui (J. Hōe), a disciple of Tz'u-ming, founded the Yang-ch'i School (J. Yōgi). Kanna Zen, or Kōan Zen as it is also termed, is Buddhist meditation practice which centers around the kōan, a brief story about an individual's search for enlightenment, often marked by irrelevancies and contradictions. This practice began to flourish under Ta-hui Tsung-kao (J. Daie Sōkō, 1089–1163), who belonged to the Lin-chi School. Quiet, meditative Zen (J. Mokushō Zen) was advocated by Hung-chih Cheng-chueh (J. Wanshi Shōkaku, 1091–1157). Kōan is a portmanteau word made from the two words *kōfu* (C. *kung-fu*, "government") and *antoku* (C. *an-tu*, "records, legal case") and indicates a precedent or model. The word "government" lends authority to the precedent. The kōan is a convenient exercise for the student to practice in a monastery. However, when this comes to be practiced generally, it exposes Buddhism to the danger of becoming a patchwork structure made up of nothing but kōan built upon kōan and may lead to the loss of the vital spirit of Sudden Enlightenment and Direct Entrance (J. *tongo jikinyū*). The quiet, meditative

Zen of Hung-chih teaches that meditation and wisdom are inseparable and that practice and enlightenment are identical. But one misstep and the entire religious practice becomes as lifeless as a withered tree and falls into quietism. The Sung Dynasty was marked by a tendency to synthesize Confucianism, Buddhism and Taoism. This syncretic tendency also made itself felt in Buddhist monasteries by movements toward the unification of Zen practice and Chinese philosophy and of Zen and Pure Land thought, which resulted in the decline of Zen. Fortunately, however, before this decline set in, Zen had been transplanted in Japan where it stimulated a unique cultural growth which may be aptly termed Zen Culture.

4.

Zen and Oriental Culture

Zen originated in the forests of India. Meditation in the cool refreshing forests was, to the Indians, an easy and pleasant way to attain to an understanding of truth. As we have already stated, Indian culture was primarily philosophical and religious. It can be seen from the Prakrit original of the Japanese term Zen, *jhāna* (C. *ch'an*, Skt. *dhyāna*), "quiet meditation" or "meditative practice," that there is a strong intellectual and philosophical coloring in Zen. This meditation formed the basis for all religious practice from which Buddhist thought developed. Accordingly, Indian Buddhism is very rich in its philosophical content. Meditation quiets the waves (distractions) of the heart-mind and enables us to see clearly the real form of all things. This serene reflection meditation is also termed *shikan* in Japanese, literally, "to stop and see." "Stop" refers to the cessation of all afflictions and distractions and therefore refers to Zen meditation in a narrow sense, while "see" means the ability to grasp the real nature of all things in their correct form and corresponds to wisdom in a narrow sense. *Shikan* in its widest sense means serene reflection meditation, for wisdom is considered an inherent part of meditation. Although wisdom refers to the wisdom of religious experience, it does not exclude the acceptance of scientific knowledge.

After Zen was transplanted in China, it was influenced by the practical culture of the Chinese, revealing characteristics hitherto unseen in India and finally was successful in establishing itself as an independent school. Chinese *ch'an* was not merely a kind of quiet meditation after the Indian style, but an enlightenment practice which points directly at the True Nature of original enlightenment (J. *hongaku shinshō*) inherent within us. Its spirit extended to the daily life of the people and finally led to the creation of the *Ch'ing-kuei* (monastic rules of etiquette) drawn from the Precepts of Buddhism (J. *ritsu*) and the ceremonies of Confucianism (C. *li*, J. *rei*). Zen was well suited to the practical nature of the Chinese people and rapidly spread throughout China. Architecture, sculpture, painting, calligraphy and pottery all developed around the *ch'an* temple.

Zen practice, once introduced into Japan, was able to blend well with the emotional element in Japanese culture and made remarkable developments. Its first task was the conversion and education of the warrior caste, among whom it later aroused the famed *Bushidō* (Way of the Warrior) spirit so characteristic of Japanese culture. Zen was a firm protector of Japanese culture at the end of the Kamakura Period

(1192–1333) when the peace was almost continuously broken by the many civil disturbances which were occurring one after another. A distinct culture, based on a practice of Zen meditation, arose which embraced such varied cultural aspects as architecture, sculpture, painting, calligraphy, landscape gardening, *Noh* drama, *renga* poetry, *haiku* poetry, pottery, *koto*, *shakuhachi* music and the tea ceremony. Zen training emphasizes concrete action rather than speculative thought and, believing that life and death are complementary to each other (J. *shōji ichinyo*), aims at overcoming them. It admires bold actions and is content with plain, simple living with due importance attached to the proper observance of ceremony and etiquette. This attitude of Zen could not help but influence the life of the warrior (J. *samurai*).

The warrior families were closely connected with politics in general without drawing a distinction between the central government and local feudal governments. The prevailing political theories of the day belonged to the Chu-tzu School (J. Shushi) which is a school of Confucianism that developed under the influence of Zen. Likewise, in the Yang-ming School (J. Yōmei) of philosophy which arose during the Ming Dynasty, there is also a marked Zen influence. The Kanazawa Library and Ashikaga College are also the fruit of this mingling of Zen and Confucianism. The Gosan Literature (learning pursued in the five great Zen monasteries of Kyōto during a period of literary decline throughout the country) was also a product of the close relationship between Confucianism and Zen. Throughout the Kamakura, Yoshino and Muromachi Periods priests of the Zen School were actively engaged in publishing the sayings of their masters (J. *goroku*), biographies of famous priests, works on the genealogical succession of priests, poetry, works on poetical rhyme, etc., thereby making a great contribution to Japanese culture. The so-called Gosan Editions are representative of this. These Editions were produced in large Zen monasteries in Kyōto and Kamakura from the beginning of the Kamakura Period to the end of the Ashikaga Period.

There are many different styles of architecture observable in the construction of Zen temples. In its early stages the Zen temple consisted of the meditation hall (J. *sōdō*), lecture hall (J. *hattō*), priests' dormitory (J. *shūryo*), master's room (J. *hōjō*), etc., but later a hall dedicated to the Buddha (J. *Butsuden*) was added, resulting in the emergence of the "Seven-hall monastery" (J. *shichidō garan*). Japanese architecture belongs largely to the style called *shoin-zukuri* whose origin is to be found in the Buddhist monastery. The characteristic entrance of the Japanese house (J. *genkan*) is copied from the gateway of the guest house (J. *kakuden*) of the Zen monastery. The Shari Hall of the Enkaku Temple in Kamakura is a representative work of the pure Karayō style and as such is very important. The Manpuku Temple at Uji presents a most interesting blend of

Ming Dynasty Temple architecture with Japanese architectural ideals.

Eisai Zenji introduced tea into Japan from China and used it chiefly as a medicine. Gradually, however, with the passing of time it came to be enjoyed more and more for its refined taste. The tea ceremony was founded by Murata Shuko (died 1502). It was systematized by Sen-no-Rikyū (1518–1591). The tea ceremony was also called *Zen-cha*, "Zen-tea," or *wabi-cha,* "wabi (i.e., elegant simplicity) tea." The tea room (J. *chashitsu*) is patterned after the ten foot square room of Yuima (Skt. *Vimalakīrti*) described in the *Yuima Kyō* (Skt. *Vimalakīrti Nirdeśa Sūtra*). The meditative spirit seen in the utensils employed in the ceremony is characterized by profundity combined with simplicity. The host and the guest blend with the universe while they are in the tea room and experience the bliss that comes from knowing the unity between oneself and others. The etiquette of the tea ceremony borrowed heavily from the "Rules for the Serving of Tea" (J. Gyōcha Shiki) of the Zen *Ch'ing-kuei.* The essential mental attitude for the performance of the tea ceremony is summed up in four words: harmony, respect, purity and tranquility (J. *wakeiseijaku*), which also appear in the Zen Manual, "Regulations of the Tea room" (J. Chabō Shingi).

The paintings found in the tea room are simple, and the characteristic blank space is made to assume meaning. Zen

India ink painting has its origin here. The number of Zen artists is very great, but among them perhaps the best known is Sesshū (1420–1506), who deeply realized the significance of the saying "Zen and art are one" (J. *Zen-ga ichimi*). He studied under Nyosetsu of the Shōkoku Temple and the disciple of Nyosetsu, Shūbun. Later he went to China where he was influenced by Hsia-kuei (J. Kakei). It is no exaggeration to say that his work surpasses that of his teachers. We find the simple, profound, pure spirit of meditation at its highest artistic expression in Sesshū's powerful, emotional, harmonious *haboku* landscape representations of nature. His head and shoulder portraits of Zen masters are also highly respected in the Zen School and show remarkable progress over other artists of his period.

Calligraphy is essentially beauty of line and is now attracting a broad interest. Many of the famous calligraphers such as Sesson, Mokuan and Ryōkan were Zen monks. Their talent and personalities are closely entwined. Calligraphy is attracting an ever-increasing interest among the people today.

The placing of flowers in the tea room gave a great impulse to the development of flower arrangement as an art. The tea room respects *sabi* (a kind of elegant simplicity) which is free from limitations. This respect for the unlimited is responsible for the development of landscape gardening, the essence of which is the employment of a seemingly distant landscape and the concealment of all traces of artificiality. The

Myōgetsu Temple of Kamakura and the Daitoku, Saihō, Tenryū and Ryōan Temples of Kyōto are famous still today as outstanding examples of landscape gardening. Many of these were laid out under the immediate direction of Zen priests.

The texts for the *Noh* drama are called in Japan *yōkyoku* and were collected and arranged by Kan'ami, Zeami, Komparu Zenchiku, Komparu Zempō and others. The present world of dreams and phantasms is the subject of the *Noh* drama. The texts are concise and abound in references to Buddhist teachings which have their real significance outside the meaning of the word itself.

Renga poetry was developed in the Ashikaga Period by Nijō Yoshimoto, Imagawa Ryōshun, Bontō, Chion, Shinkei and others. The Zen spirit completely dominated their lives. The ultimate ideal of poetry and the spirit of Zen are at one: self-enlightenment without a teacher[*] (J. *mushi dokugo*), experiencing the real feeling of things (literally, knowing hot and cold by oneself, J. *reidan-jichi*) and sudden, direct enlightenment (J. *tongo jikishō*). *Renga* poetry is a kind of Japanese poetry composed by two or more people. Because agreement

---

[*] The Buddha made it clear that he was not a savior, that each person must find the Truth for himself or herself. However, in the Serene Reflection Meditation tradition emphasis is put on the master-disciple relationship as the most effective means of giving up the self and as the vehicle of spiritual transmission.

between two poets is necessary to compose a *renga*, its essence lies in perfect harmony.

Another characteristic form of Japanese poetry is *haiku*, which despite its brevity, is capable of reflecting the entire universe in a split second. The accompanying profound mental attitude is in perfect accord with the understanding that comes from the practice of meditation. The superb *haiku* by Bashō are quite unintelligible without an understanding of Buddhist meditation practice.

Formerly, before entering a tea ceremony room, it was customary to play the *koto* (a kind of musical instrument). Tung-kao Hsin-yueh (J. Tōkō Shin'etsu, 1642–1696), who came to Japan from China during the Tokugawa Period, was an expert calligrapher, artist and musician. He especially excelled in the playing of the *koto* and composed twenty-four pieces. The hooded, itinerant priests of the Fuke Zen School developed the Kaikō and Kōkō pieces and were renowned for their skill in playing the flute (J. *shakuhachi*). The lingering notes of the flute eloquently point toward the profundity of meditation.

It goes without saying that pottery received a great impulse from the tea ceremony. The founder of Japanese pottery making, Katō Kagemasa, crossed over to China in the company of Dōgen Zenji, the First Ancestor of the Japanese Sōtō School. He may be considered a pioneer in Japanese *setomono* (pottery).

The architecture and sculpture of the Zen monastery do not have gaudy embellishments, but rather take a simple form, the total effect being graceful and unfettered. This may be regarded as a material expression of the meditative spirit.

To quote *Life* magazine, "Zen is an austere sect which seeks truth by meditation and intuition." Zen in its earnestness is closer to Theravāda Buddhism (the form of Buddhism practiced in Southeast Asia) than any other school of Mahāyāna Buddhism. Zen followers attach more importance to practical actions than to the study of the Scriptures. In Zen all actions must be simple and yet have depth. This ideal of simplicity exerted a great influence on Japanese art and life.

The chief characteristics of art based on Buddhist meditation practice are simplicity and strength, a wealth of vitality, complete union with nature and the ability to break through any confinement which might prove restrictive. This art permeated every aspect of Japanese culture and, by aiming at profundity and simplicity, has made for itself a permanent place in the world of art. Because of the Zen ideals of simplicity and intuitive inspiration, it is now exciting the interest of European and American intellectuals and artists. The famous psychoanalyst Carl Jung included Zen in his "Archetypes," comparing individuation and Zen enlightenment. The French modern artist Braque declared that he painted by "flashes of Zen." Zen practice has now crossed the sea and is drawing the attention of

Westerners. Influenced by Buddhist meditation, the Japanese culture which rests upon the ideals of *wabi* and *sabi* (simplicity and elegance) has produced a unique art and given great tranquility and refinement to the people. It is only natural that the Western world, hitherto completely in the grip of a mechanical civilization, will, through contact with art and culture which grew out of Buddhist meditation, find it possible to return to the source of life. [Editor's comment: Eastern forms are not superior to Western forms. The forms themselves are empty. The significance of this is that if one actually meditates, all of one's work will be an expression of that practice. Many Westerners who study Buddhism get caught thinking that the Oriental form is important or superior to Western form, which it is not.]

5.

The Basic Meaning of Sōtō Zen

The name Sōtō is derived from the first character in the names of two of its masters, Tōzan Ryōkai (C. Tung-shan Liang-chieh) and Sōzan Honjaku (C. Ts'ao-shan Pen-chi). In the "Sayings of Tōzan" (J. Tōzan Goroku), it is written, "As the profound style of Tōzan made itself felt in all parts of the Empire, Zen masters, in order to show their respect for Tōzan, called the school the Tōsō School." Thus the school was first known as Tōsō, but perhaps for euphonic reasons, the characters in the name were later reversed to read "Sōtō." In the "Thesis on the Ten Regulations of the School" (C. Tsung-men Shih-kuei-lun, J. Shūmon Jikki Ron) by Fa-yen (J. Hōgen), the Sōtō School is placed alongside the Rinzai and Igyō Schools. The above-mentioned work was written between 940 and 950 C.E. Prior to that, Hōgen, the author, had roamed about the country and heard the school names Rinzai, Igyō and Sōtō from Buddhist scholars. Thus it is clear that the name Sōtō was already in use by 910 or 920 C.E.

Sōzan died in 901 C.E., Ungo Dōyō the following year and Ryūge Kyoton (C. Lung-ya Chu-tun) in 923 C.E. It is also known that the name Sōtō was already in use soon after the deaths of Sōzan and Ungo and before the death of Ryūge.

Fun'yō Zenshō (C. Fen-yang Shan-chao) refers to the school as the Tōzan School or the Tōjo School. It thus would appear that the name Sōtō was not used by members of the school, but rather by outsiders. Tōzan had many disciples besides Sōzan Honjaku. Therefore, the Zen of Tōzan was not only transmitted through the line of Sōzan, but also through the line of another of his famous disciples, Ungo Dōyō. The line of Sōzan terminated after only four generations. The present-day Sōtō school represents the line of Ungo. Therefore the Sōtō School may also be called the Ungo Branch of Zen. It is not correct to limit the Zen of Sōtō, then, merely to Tōzan and Sōzan as the name would imply.

Another theory states that the Sō in Sōtō refers not to Sōzan, but to the Sixth Ancestor, who is also known as Sōkei Enō. Sōzan was a devout admirer of the Sixth Ancestor and as an expression of his admiration adopted the first character in the name of the Sixth Ancestor for use in his own name. Thus even if the Sō in Sōtō refers to Sōzan, indirectly it still refers back to Sōkei, the Sixth Ancestor. There are those within the Sōtō School who reject the idea that Sō indirectly points to the Sixth Ancestor, steadfastly maintaining that the character Sō was chosen for the school name directly from the name of the Sixth Ancestor without the intercession of Sōzan. This view is derived more from religious faith than from historical accuracy. Great Master Dōgen, who first introduced Sōtō Zen into Japan, states from the standpoint of religion that the Japanese Sōtō School is the direct recipient of the line of the Sixth Ancestor through the line of Tōzan and is not merely one more of the many schools of Zen. Dōgen calls the Sixth Ancestor and Tōzan "venerable Buddhas," but makes no such allusion to Sōzan. Neither Ejō nor Gikai in Japan seems to make use of the appellation "Sōtō." It probably came into use after Great Master Keizan. According to both Great Master Keizan and an Imperial Rescript presented to Sōji-ji, the name Sōtō was compounded from the name of the Sixth Ancestor and of Tōzan.

The Sōtō School in China made little showing in its early years of development. However, its popularity had greatly increased by the middle of the Sung Dynasty. Its main characteristics were: 1) that all beings have the Buddha Nature at birth and consequently are essentially enlightened, 2) that one can enjoy fully the Bliss of the Buddha Nature through the practice of serene reflection meditation (Zazen), 3) that training and enlightenment are identical and 4) that the strict discipline of the religious ceremonies and temple regulations must be internalized and applied to our everyday activities.

The line of succession from Tōzan to Dōgen is as follows: Tōzan Ryōkai, Ungo Dōyō, Dōan Dōhi, Dōan Kanshi, Ryōzan

Enkan, Daiyō Kyōgen, Tōsu Gisei, Fuyō Dōkai, Tanka Shijun, Chōro Seiryō, Tendō Sōkaku, Setchō Chikan, Tendō Nyojō, Eihei Dōgen. (The names above are given only in their Japanese pronunciation.) The first four Ancestors lived in the area of Nan-ch'ang (J. Nanshō). Ryozan lived to the west of Tung-t'ing (J. Dōtei) Lake where he increased the strength of the school. Daiyō taught Sōtō Zen in the vicinity of Hsiang-yang (J. Shōyō). Tōsu settled in the area between Nanking and Chiu-chiang (J. Kyūkō), i.e., in the area of An-ching (J. Ankei) carrying the teaching to the southeast. Fuyō spread Zen in Lo-yang (J. Rakuyō) and Kai-feng (J. Kaifū). Tanka remained only in the North Mountains proclaiming the law of direct, awakened enlightenment. Chōro went South to I-cheng (J. Gicho) in Chiangsu (J. Kōso) Province and, later moving to Chekiang (J. Sekkō) Province, taught a variety of Zen influenced by Kegon ideas. Afterwards, Ming-chou (J. Minshū) in Chekiang Province became the center of the Sōtō School. Both Mt. T'ien-t'ung (J. Tendō) and Mt. Hsueh-tou (J. Setchō) are in Ming-chou. Chikan was by nature a simple and earnest man who traveled little. Yet we may say of him that his voice was heard throughout the empire. Nyojō (1163–1238) lived in six different places during his lifetime. Finally he settled on Mt. T'ien-t'ung at the age of sixty-two by Imperial request. He had a firm, critical attitude and taught a rigorous type of Zen, exerting a great influence on later generations.

It was Great Master Dōgen who first brought Sōtō Zen to Japan. Great Master Keizan made possible the popularization of Sōtō Zen, thereby laying the foundation for the large religious organization which it is today. Dōgen was born into a noble family. When still young, he came to know the meaning of the Buddhist word *mujō* (impermanence) through the loss of both his parents. It is only natural then that he decided to become a Buddhist priest and search for Truth. He went first to Mt. Hiei, the headquarters for the Tendai School. At the young age of fifteen, he was assailed by the following doubt: "Both the esoteric and exoteric doctrine of the Buddha teach that enlightenment is inherent in all beings from the outset; but if this is so, what causes all the Buddhas, past, present and future, to seek enlightenment if they already are enlightened?" Such a doubt, clearly pointing to the dualistic contradiction between the ideal and the actual, is a kind of anguish likely to arise in the mind of any deeply religious person. Unable to resolve this great doubt on Mt. Hiei, Dōgen decided to study Buddhism under Great Master Eisai. He practiced Rinzai meditation with Eisai's disciple, Myōzen. At the age of twenty-four Dōgen, accompanied by Myōzen, embarked on the dangerous journey to China in search of the highest truths of Buddhism. There he visited all of the well-known monasteries, finally becoming a disciple of Ju-ching (J. Nyojō) who was living on Mt. T'ien-tung (J. Tendō). Dōgen strove hard day and night for two years and at last realized the liberation of body and mind (J. *shinjin datsuraku datsuraku shinjin*), the most important event of one's life. Dōgen freed himself from the illusion of ego which arises from a dualistic way of thinking and experienced deeply the bliss of Buddhist Truth. He continued his religious training in China for two more years before returning to Japan at the age of twenty-eight. Dōgen's greatest desire was that he would be able to transmit the Buddhist teaching and thereby benefit all mankind. He first settled in Kōshō Temple, where he set himself upon the task of instructing monastic trainees. He had a training hall (J. *dōjō*) built, and he taught the Buddhist monastic Sangha and laity alike for more than ten years. In 1243, at the earnest supplication of Hatano Yoshishige, he moved to Echizen in the present-day Fukui Prefecture and founded Eihei-ji Temple, which is now one of the two head temples of the Sōtō School. Burning with great enthusiasm to teach true Buddhism to all those who were in search of it, he spent some ten years here leading a peaceful religious life.

Dōgen is the greatest religious figure and creative thinker in Japanese history. Farsighted leaders outside the Sōtō School have declared that the essence of Japanese culture cannot be correctly understood without considering this great religious teacher. Deeply impressed at the breadth and the depth of Dōgen's thought, leaders have noted Dōgen's profound and pervasive influence on Japanese culture. The reason Dōgen is so highly evaluated by scholars is because his philosophy, religion and personality are in perfect accord with the ideals held by humanity throughout history, possess broad objectivity and are universally applicable. Dōgen's greatness rests on three points: the profundity of his thought, its practicality and the loftiness of his character. His principal work, *Shōbōgenzō (The Treasure House of the Eye of the True Teaching)* in ninety-five chapters, is a true masterpiece clearly revealing his thought and faith. It is written not in classical Chinese, which was so popular in the period of Dōgen, but in the Japanese language so that all could read it. Its style is concise and to the point; his thought, noble and profound. His sharp logic and deep thought may not only be regarded as being in the forefront of Japanese philosophy, but also as occupying an important position in modern philosophy. Because of this, it is possible that it may synthesize Oriental and Occidental thought. However, the greatness of Dōgen is not found merely in the excellence of his theories. It should always be borne in mind that Dōgen does not amuse himself with intellectual speculation and barren phrases divorced from reality. In Dōgen's writings we find theory and practice, knowledge and action, inseparably entwined. The meticulous Zen regulations found in Dōgen's *Eihei Daishingi* establish this fact very clearly. Buddhism teaches that we must grasp our own body and mind thoroughly and understand them fully. This does not mean mere intellectual knowledge, but rather grasping them through intense religious training by means of which we shall find the life of the Buddha.

The greatness of Dōgen lies in the deep theory and scrupulous practice which are perfectly harmonized in his noble character. Dōgen rejected worldly honors and wealth, kept aloof from the powerful families of the day and was content to spend his life in the humble black robes of a priest. He devoted himself to the training of sincere people, however few their number might be, in the mountains of Echizen. He rejected unfounded contributions from the regent, Tokiyori, and returned purple robes sent him by the Imperial court.

Among Dōgen's many successors, the most famous are Ejō, Sōkai and Senne. The mantle of Koun Ejō passed to his disciple Tettsū Gikai and then to the Great Master, Keizan Jōkin (1268–1325). Keizan founded Sōji-ji, which is one of the two head temples of the Sōtō School. He is designated "Taisō" or Great Ancestor because he exerted great influence on later generations. There is a Japanese proverb which says, "The difficulty is not to start an enterprise, but to carry it to final success." In order to preserve what has been given to us, and to adapt this so that it can suit the needs of the times, unremitting efforts are necessary.

Keizan was born in Fukui Prefecture. At the age of six, he had already decided to become a priest and at eight became a disciple of Tettsū Zenji at Eihei-ji. He served him for about six years. He took his Bodhisattva vows (vows to save all sentient beings before enjoying his own enlightenment) under Ejō Zenji, who was his master for seven years. He keenly felt the need for actual meditation practice and at the age of nineteen sought guidance from Jakuen Zenji at Yōkyō-ji Temple. Later, he studied under Hōkaku at Manji Temple in Kyōto, Hakuun Egyō and other Zen masters, including the famous Shōichi Kokushi. He also studied the Tendai doctrine on Mt. Hiei and Zen under Hattō Kakushin. In 1289, at the age of twenty-two, he arrived at Daijō-ji in Kaga and there devoted himself whole-heartedly to the study and practice of Sōtō Zen under Tettsū Zenji. He remained at Daijō-ji for some seven years receiving the instruction of his master and reading widely in the Buddhist canon. He finally was enlightened at the age of twenty-seven in 1294 by practicing the kōan which declares, "Your ordinary heart: that's the way." He thought deeply about the meaning of the kōan and finally was able to penetrate the mind of the Master who had given him the kōan, thereby being able to taste the deepest of all religious experiences. In January of the following year, his master Tettsū conferred upon Keizan his robe as a symbol of the Transmission.

Keizan continued his religious exercises after his enlightenment, carrying out the lofty ideal of spreading the teaching of Buddhism and thereby benefiting humanity. In the autumn of 1295 he founded the Jōman-ji Temple in Awa. He visited the

Zen Master, Gi'in in Higo, Kyūshū, in the spring of 1297. In January of the year 1300, he delivered sermons before many large gatherings in place of his master at Daijō-ji Temple. After his formal inauguration as second master of Daijō-ji Temple in December 1304, clergy and laity alike flocked to him. At the invitation of Jōjū-ji Temple he became its first master in 1311. He founded Yōkō-ji Temple in Noto in 1313 and thereby laid the foundation for spreading the teachings in Kaga and Noto Provinces. In 1325 Keizan was invited by Jōken Risshi, chief priest of Shōgaku-ji Temple in Kusui, Noto, to take up residence there after Kannon (Skt. *Avalokiteśvara*) had appeared to the latter in a dream. Accordingly, in June of that year, Keizan renamed the temple Sōji-ji.

In one of the main works of Keizan, *The Record of the Transmission of the Light* (J. *Denkōroku*), it is written, "Shakyamuni held the flower aloft to let it be known that IT *was, is and will be* immutable and indestructible whilst Makakasho broke into a smile to let it be known that IT *was, is and will be* beyond beginning or end,"* which is a phrase often quoted in Zen texts and refers to the Buddha who, when asked

---

* Keizan Zenji, *The Denkōroku or The Record of the Transmission of the Light*, trans. Rev. Hubert Nearman, O.B.C., with Rev. Master P.T.N.H. Jiyu-Kennett, M.O.B.C., as consultant and editor (Mt. Shasta, California: Shasta Abbey Press, 1993), p. 8.

to give a sermon, merely held up a lotus flower in his hand. Here Keizan uses this phrase to point to the Transmission of the teachings outside the Scriptures. The "smile" refers to Makakasho, the disciple of the Buddha who signified his understanding of the uplifted flower by a faint smile. The passage from *The Denkōroku* quoted here stresses the universality of the Truth throughout all time and space. In this work Keizan expresses deep respect for Dōgen and, although endeavoring to live in his tradition, reveals originality by striking out on a new point of departure for himself. He always kept in mind the true spirit of Dōgen, yet he popularized it and adapted it to suit the needs of the times. He paid particular attention to the social aspect of religion and strove hard with an all-embracing spirit to train his many disciples. His popularization of the teachings of the Sōtō School and genius for administration caused the school to flourish and laid the basis for its present-day success. His successors drew the common people to the school by their strict adherence to the ideals set forth by Dōgen and through active missionary work in all parts of Japan and before all classes of people.

In summary, the essence of Sōtō Zen is: 1) to ground yourself with an unwavering practice of meditation and not be sidetracked by the petty demands of greed and anger, 2) to wholeheartedly seek the way of Truth by utterly forsaking all desires for fame and gain, 3) to live in Truth, avoiding the company of those who pursue wealth and power, 4) to practice meditation and to perfect religious training for the sake of training, 5) to teach the necessity of continuous religious training and enlightenment which are one and the same thing, 6) to transmit correctly the Teaching of the Buddha and Ancestors from master to disciple and to cause this Transmission to grow ever wider, 7) to harmonize theory and practice and not to cling to either the ideal or the actual and 8) to express our gratitude by diligent application of our religious practice in every activity of our daily life.

6.

The True Spirit of the Two Ancestors

The Japanese Sōtō School was firmly established with the Highest Ancestor Great Master Dōgen as its dignified father and the Greatest Ancestor Great Master Keizan as its compassionate mother. The Transmission of the Dharma from master to disciple in the Sōtō School is a matter of extreme importance. It has two aspects: the horizontal and the vertical. The former emphasizes the sameness between master and disciple, and the latter recognizes their respective individualities.

Dōgen received the Dharma Transmission from his master, Ju-ching (J. Tendō Nyojō), yet he revealed his own individuality and opened up a new field of thought in Buddhism. Dōgen selected what was best in Buddhism regardless of school and tried to return to the basic spirit of the Buddha. He cast aside worldly honors and wealth, avoided the powerful, prosperous people of his day and never wore any elegant robes, but only ones made of coarse material. He worked diligently to train the few monks around him. He denied the theory that Buddhism, Confucianism and Taoism are in essence the same and rejected the idea which holds that there are five schools of Zen, advocating a unified Buddhism to the point that he disliked even using the name Zen School. Insofar as he was enlightened under Ju-ching, we can say that his spiritual understanding and that of Ju-ching were the same.

Dōgen developed his own individuality with this tradition as a background:

1. The essence of the teachings of Dōgen lies, first of all, in the correct Transmission of a unified Buddhism. If the Zen School forms its own system in contrast to those of other schools, it is apt to become one-sided and biased. Dōgen, in rejecting the name Zen School as indicating something distinct from other schools, said, "Those who use the name Zen School to describe the great Way of the Buddha and the Ancestors have not yet seen the Way of the Buddha. The establishment of the five schools of Zen is nothing other than the destruction of the unity of Buddhism. It is the product of shallow thinking." Dōgen sought to restore sectarian Sung Dynasty Zen to the main road of Buddhism from which it had strayed and to enable Chinese Buddhism which had deviated from the main course to find itself again.

Great Master Keizan also rejected the sectarian concept of five schools of Zen by declaring in his *Denkōroku:* "People need not debate about the five or seven schools of Zen, but rather should merely brighten their own hearts. This is the correct teaching of all the Buddhas. Why do people always engage in controversy? It is a waste of time to discuss the idea of victory or defeat." In order to find true Buddhism there must be an urgent desire to find the Truth. In the *Shōbōgenzō Zuimonki* Great Master Dōgen says: "If one has a real desire to enter Buddhism, then one must not hesitate to go to a master for training even if it means such difficulties as crossing the seas and climbing mountains. However, even if we should go and urge those who have no desire to enter Buddhism, it cannot be certain whether or not they will accept it." Dōgen, who was free from egotism and vain desires for fame and gain, rejected the Buddhism of his period as something imperfect. It goes without saying that in selecting which of the teachings of Buddhism are to be spread throughout the land, the time, the place and the persons to receive the teachings must be taken into consideration.

The division of the teachings of Buddhism into three periods (the period of the True Law, the period of the imitation of the True Law and the period of decline of the True Law) is nothing but a skillful means (Skt. *upāya*, J. *hōben*) to explain the changes in Buddhist teachings to those who have not yet directly experienced the Truth. Precisely because we are now in the period of decline, we must make unrelenting efforts to live in the spirit of the Buddha and to grasp the essence of Buddhism directly. Therefore Dōgen said: "If you do not enter Buddhism in this life on the pretext that we are in a period of decline and unable to know Truth, then in which life will you realize

Truth?" Dōgen emphasized the efforts of people to discover the Eternal within themselves. We can observe here Dōgen's intense resistance to religious fatalism and the idea that it was not possible to find the Truth during a period of decline in the Buddhist teaching. If one has a sincere desire to seek Truth, then the limitations of time and place can be transcended, and one can see the Buddha and Ancestors directly. This is because the three periods referred to above are not periods in time, but are really stages in the development of men. Great Master Keizan stated in his *Denkōroku*: "There is no time boundary between the three periods. This is true in India, China, and Japan alike. Therefore do not bewail the coming of the period of decline. Do not be prejudiced against those from distant places and remote areas." He respects the heroic spirit which casts off the spell of "the period of decline" and boldly goes forth in the search for true Buddhism.

2. The standpoint taken by Great Master Dōgen is new in that it does not handle the problems of the Buddhist Scriptures in an academic, objective way, but delves into each one as if it were a problem presented to Dōgen personally. Although the Buddhism which bases itself upon Scripture as final authority has great depth, it often falls into a mere intellectual Buddhism unable to transform itself into a living religion. Dōgen's Buddhism is based upon wholehearted Zazen which rejects the dualism of mind and matter and holds that the training process

involved in formal seated meditation is enlightenment. But as long as one plays with mental discriminations of good and bad, right and wrong, as intellectual ideas, it will be impossible to find the True Way of the Buddha. Dōgen said, "Attainment of the Way can only be achieved with one's body." The formal seated meditation is the attainment of Buddhahood through our body. It is life and vitality itself. It is commonly said that enlightenment is the ideal of serene reflection meditation, and that serene reflection meditation is the means for the attainment of that ideal. But, as explained before, meditation can never be considered merely a means to an end.

Dōgen rejects the duality of enlightenment and the religious training of meditation, writing in "Bendōwa" (a chapter of the *Shōbōgenzō*): "It is heretical to believe that training and enlightenment are separable for, in Buddhism, the two are one and the same. Since training embraces enlightenment, the very beginning of training contains the whole of original enlightenment; as this is so, the teacher tells his disciples never to search for enlightenment outside of training since the latter mirrors enlightenment." [Quoted from *Zen is Eternal Life*, 1999 edition, p. 186.] Just-sitting meditation based on faith is the fullest form of true enlightenment. The world of religion is absolute in that it rejects the categories of means and end, for it is its own end. Today is not something for tomorrow, but remains absolute as today. Therefore, Great Master Dōgen declared that wholehearted meditation is neither a practice in which one waits for enlightenment such as was found in the Sung Dynasty in China, nor is it a means to become Buddha. Enlightenment is an inherent part of meditation practice from the outset. Just-sitting meditation is free from all obstacles and is synonymous with enlightenment. We call this meditation in enlightenment and enlightenment in meditation. *Kekka-fuza* (sitting cross-legged with the soles of both feet turned upward) is the *samādhi* (meditation) practiced by all the Buddhas in which they alone fully enjoy the bliss derived therefrom.

Formal seated meditation is not considered an unpleasant, compulsory religious exercise, but an act of the Buddhas which is in perfect harmony with nature and in accord with the spirit of the Buddha. Zazen, always surrounded by the twin ideas of training and enlightenment, is in itself complete enlightenment and the bodily posture which reveals the fullest manifestation of this Original Enlightenment. It is a religious exercise, and yet at the same time it is the state of Great Enlightenment. Serene reflection meditation, from which nothing is sought and nothing is gained (J. *mushotoku mushogo no Zazen*), must never be construed to mean a denial of practice itself, because to deny religious practice would result in being unable to unite it with theory. Dōgen says in the "Bendōwa," "Both the Buddhas and Ancestors insisted upon the necessity of intense training in order that enlightenment may be kept pure, being identical with training itself." [*Zen is Eternal Life*, 1999 edition, p. 187.] Since these practices correspond to Original Enlightenment, they are unending. As a result of realizing enlightenment, we continue to meditate; as a result of realizing Buddhahood, we continue to train. Serene reflection meditation, which is the complete liberation of body and mind, means that the whole of oneself becomes the Dharma and living embodiment of the Buddhas and Ancestors.

Great Master Keizan wrote in his "Zazen Yojinki," "The true mind of meditation is not one which waits for enlightenment," and in his *Denkōroku*, "The performance of meritorious deeds not free from the laws of karma (cause and effect, J. *ui kugō*), will not lead to untainted Buddhahood. If we seek Buddhahood we must return to the source of life. Religious practice which waits for enlightenment does not lead to Buddhahood." Thus, Great Master Keizan, like Great Master Dōgen, rejected the Sung idea of a meditation practice which strives for enlightenment, maintaining that serene reflection meditation is an absolutely pure religious exercise which in and of itself expresses Buddhahood.

3. It is natural that the Buddhist religion which rejects the idea of an absolute God should declare that the essence of the Buddha, i.e., the Buddha Nature, is found in all men. Because Buddha Nature exists in all beings, It allows those who train to realize enlightenment. The practice of serene reflection

meditation is a manifestation of faith in the Buddha Nature. Zazen, which teaches the identity between enlightenment and training, becomes the preliminary step for the realization of enlightenment. Buddhism in general teaches that there is a gradual development toward enlightenment which is made possible because of the Buddha Nature. However, serene reflection meditation is in perfect harmony with Original Enlightenment itself which is the Buddha Nature. Yet simultaneously it transforms itself into this enlightenment and causes it to materialize fully. Enlightenment and serene reflection meditation are identical. The teaching that Original Enlightenment is found in all beings is the essence of Zen.

This view of the Buddha Nature is unique to Great Master Dōgen and reveals a new approach unobservable in other schools of Buddhism. There is a famous passage in the *Nehan Gyō (Nirvāna Sūtra)* which reads: "All beings have the Buddha Nature." However, Dōgen interprets this as "All beings *are* the Buddha Nature!" emphasizing that the Buddha Nature is the basis of all existence and the source of all that is of value. In "Busshō-no-Maki," a chapter of the *Shōbōgenzō*, Dōgen explains: "The Buddha Nature is everything, one part of which we call humanity. Within humanity and outside of it everything is the Buddha Nature." All things which exist are part of the sea of the Buddha Nature. We are apt to think of the Buddha Nature as something deep and unfamiliar, but it is nothing more than "the chin of a donkey or mouth of a horse," to quote Dōgen. All existing things are themselves manifestations of the Buddha Nature and must be the self-expression of the Buddha Nature. From this basic problem Dōgen then proceeded to a thorough discussion of the existent Buddha Nature, the non-existent Buddha Nature, the explanatory Buddha Nature and the impermanent Buddha Nature. Although all existence comes under the heading of the Buddha Nature, the definition of Buddha Nature cannot be limited merely to existence alone. It transcends this and moves on to another new world. This is an unending denial of denial, an expansion into the infinite. Therefore, absolute non-existence which includes both relative existence and non-existence is in itself the Buddha Nature. Non-existence is the source of the form without a form. The Buddha Nature itself has no form, and yet it can manifest itself in all forms. The explanation of the Buddha Nature according to Dōgen means that the Buddha Nature itself explains its True Nature as it is. The formless Buddha Nature reveals its own figure through phenomena which have form. Existence is not something fixed, immovable; non-existence is not a vacuum, not empty, but immaculate.

Impermanence which transcends existence and non-existence is the growth and development of the infinite. It is impermanence which is the true form of the Buddha Nature and the self-development of it. The impermanent Buddha Nature regenerates itself constantly and thereby keeps on growing and extending itself throughout time and space. Great Master Keizan declares in his *Shinjin-mei Nentei*: "There are two kinds of Buddha Nature: the existent one (J. *u*) and the non-existent one (J. *mu*). The non-existent one is indivisible; the existent one has not a fixed, unchanging existence." Also he observes, "Buddha comes forth in the world; things appear in the hearts of men. The Buddhas of the many countries conceal their physical bodies revealing only their shadows. The countries of the various Buddhas reveal their forms completely." Thus does Keizan uphold Dōgen's idea that "the Buddha Nature is everything" as well as Dōgen's four-way analysis of the Buddha Nature. It is further stated in the "Zazen Yōjinki" that Zazen illuminates the mind of man and enables him to live peacefully in his True Self. We call this "showing your natural face" or "revealing the natural scenery," thus making clear the content of enlightenment and the religious practice of the Buddha Heart.

4. Dōgen, after being assailed by the doubts described above while he was on Mt. Hiei, came to the conclusion that despite the extent of Buddhist studies in Japan, the true Buddhism was still unknown. He therefore resolved to go to China to find it, confident that he would be successful if he sought the true Buddhism from the standpoint that all Buddhism is one. However, what Dōgen sought was not a

theoretical solution, but religious peace of mind. In China he visited famous Buddhist scholars in Liang-che (J. Ryōsetsu) and studied under masters of the five schools of Zen, but to no avail. They could not satisfy his longings for religious Truth and dispel the doubts that assailed him. At last he became a disciple of Ju-ching under whose guidance he arrived at the liberation of body and mind, thereby freeing himself from all doubts. This deep experience became a source from which a new Buddhism emerged which had been Transmitted from teacher to disciple. Of this Dōgen said: "In liberating my mind and body, I preserved the traditions of ancestral succession even after I returned to Japan."

Correctly transmitted Buddhism means that the spirit of Gautama Buddha, the historic founder of Buddhism, is alive in the personalities of the successive Ancestors and Masters and that this Buddhism is pure and its practice of the Way of the Buddha perfect. It is not prejudiced in favor of the recorded word of the Buddha, or biased in favor of his mind, but rather accepts the Buddha as a complete entity, mind and body. Dōgen fervently wished to grasp the essential source of Buddhism, rejecting its many branches and schools in order to enable it to flourish. But, in the final analysis, what is it that gives a firm foundation to Buddhism? To this we must answer that it is the uninterrupted direct succession from master to disciple (J. *menju shihō*). In this direct succession (*menju*) the personalities of master and disciple are fused into one; the spirit being handed on from one person to the next is without interruption. This Transmission is not based on historical studies, but stands firmly on deep faith.

Buddhism which lives in faith must necessarily have its basis in strength derived from personality. The life of the Tathagata (Buddha) is preserved in fact only when there is an uninterrupted union of personalities between Gautama, the historic Buddha, and the unbroken line of Ancestors. This Transmission resembles the pouring of water from one vessel to another in that the true spirit of the Buddha is passed on to the next Ancestor without increasing nor decreasing. The whole character of the Buddha as it is becomes the character of the Ancestor suited to the time and place of that Ancestor. This is the reason, therefore, that the successive Ancestors all live in the character of the Buddha. It is therefore said, "Your (obvious) face is not your real one. The real one is transmitted from the Buddha." When the false self dies within us, we find our life in that of the Buddha. The Buddha and those who live in his spirit are identical no matter how many centuries or generations may separate them. In this way the life of the Buddha continues throughout history, adapting itself to time and place. To return to the source of Buddhism also means to project oneself into the future. Real traditions which live throughout history are continuously developing.

The Denkōroku by Great Master Keizan is a skillfully written work which recounts the enlightenment stories of the Ancestors. In it is found the famous phrase: "By taking a flower Shakyamuni showed that TRUTH *was, is and will be* eternal and by smiling He pointed out that it *was, is and will be* endless," explained at the end of Chapter Two. It further states, "Therefore the warm flesh of Shakyamuni is now and always here and the smiling of Makakasho is now and always new." [*Zen is Eternal Life*, 1999, pp. 229–230.] The warmth of Shakyamuni's body was correctly transmitted through the individuality of his disciple Makakasho; the true face of the Highest Ancestor (Dōgen) was handed down through the Greatest Ancestor (Keizan).

5. The basic thought and faith of Dōgen and Keizan are in perfect agreement with each other. However, differences in individuality, environment and time resulted in separate approaches to the question of how to propagate their religion. Dōgen's personality was very serious, his theory precise. The Japanese Sōtō School is proud to have such a truly great man as its founder. It would be difficult to find another Zen master who is endowed with the same profundity of thought, seriousness of practice and loftiness of character as Dōgen.

In religion, on the one hand, we must go forward ever deepening our religious experiences, while, on the other hand, recognizing our mission to guide other people to the depths of our own experience. We must enable them to know the joy that comes from a knowledge of the Dharma and the bliss that comes from the practice of meditation. It is absolutely essential to have a personal character like that of Great Master Keizan in order to carry out this mission. To regard all people with warm affection, to become the friend of the common people, to enter the realm of the ideal together with them and to share one's joy with others—these are the characteristics of the true man of religion. The Sōtō School believes that it is able to fulfill its basic mission because of the stern, father-like character of Dōgen and the compassionate mother-like character of Keizan. The foundation of the Sōtō School was laid by Dōgen. Keizan deserves the credit for shaping the monastic priesthood and broadening the social outlook of the school. The monastic priesthood developed because the foundation set by Dōgen was coupled with maintenance by Keizan.

In summary, we may say that although there was no difference in the basic spirit of the two Ancestors, they did possess distinct personalities. This was revealed in many ways: the deep philosophy of Dōgen contrasted with the clear explanations of it by Keizan, the select few who were the disciples of Dōgen compared with the multitude who benefitted from Keizan. Dōgen's religious life was characterized by sternness, whereas that of Keizan showed a magnanimous attitude which embraced all people. The former established the school while the latter displayed the administrative genius necessary for it to flourish. In the Sōtō School the two Ancestors are compared to the two wheels of a cart, for if one is lacking, the other is of little use in fulfilling its ultimate purpose. That we of the Sōtō School should have two such great men as Founders of our school is, we feel, most fortunate and significant in terms of Buddhist karma.

7.

The Key to the Doctrines of the Sōtō School and to the Pacification of the Mind

It is written in the Scriptures that one should enter Buddhism through faith. But this does not apply only to Buddhism; all religions begin and end with faith. The basic principle of the religious reformation carried out by Luther was summed up by the phrase: "only through faith" (*allein durch die Glauben*). It is inner faith, not 'good works,' which will save mankind. In Buddhism it is generally thought that it is the Pure Land Teaching (belief in salvation through faith in Amida Buddha) that emphasizes pacification of the mind through faith. However, the doctrine of faith is not something which is limited to the Pure Land School. The Buddhism of the Kamakura Period, particularly faith in the Original Vow of the Buddha as taught by Shinran, invocation of the *Lotus Sūtra* as taught by Nichiren, realization of one's innate enlightenment as taught by Dōgen, are all examples of teachings based on faith. It is no exaggeration to say that the peace of mind which is the object of the school is impossible without faith. Dōgen says, "If one has correct faith in one's heart, then one must undergo religious training and begin to study the teaching." Further, "Where faith appears, the Buddha and Ancestors appear," and "The way to dispel illusion can only be found with the help of correct faith." Great Master Keizan says in his *Shinjin-mei Nentei*, "Once correct faith has been awakened in one, who shall worry about not having entered upon the road of religion? If doubt is not dispelled, it will never really be possible to enter upon the true road." But what is this correct faith? We think it consists of three things: taking refuge in Shakyamuni Buddha, practicing serene reflection meditation, which is the realization of our inherent enlightenment, and religious training which is the expression of our gratitude. The object of veneration, the Buddha, is the source whence our teaching is derived and the guarantor of our belief and therefore has the greatest significance in our school. At the conclusion of the *Shushōgi* by Dōgen it is written, "All the Buddhas are within the one Buddha Shakyamuni, and all the Buddhas of past, present and future become Shakyamuni Buddha when they reach Buddhahood." In Buddhist doctrine we often come across such Buddhas as Amida (Skt. *Amitabha*), Dainichi (Skt. *Mahāvairocana*) and others. However, these are only manifestations of Shakyamuni Buddha.

History informs us that Shakyamuni became a monk at twenty-nine and realized enlightenment at thirty-five. As Buddhist thought developed and expanded, many others likewise attained enlightenment. Both Mahāyāna and Hinayāna consider the origin of Buddhism to be in Buddhagaya (the place where the Buddha attained enlightenment). We may therefore say that the object of veneration of the Sōtō School is Shakyamuni Buddha who attained enlightenment under the Bodhi tree in Buddhagaya and who is the model for all Buddhas. He is neither a Buddha conjured up in the imagination, nor an idealized Buddha devoid of a real personality, but an actual historical person. Later generations viewed the nature (body) of a Buddha from three different aspects: 1) The Body of the Law (Skt. *Dharmakāya*, J. *Hosshin*) which is a personification of the True Laws of the Universe and hence transcending all finite limitations; 2) The Body of Bliss (Skt. *Sambhogakāya*, J. *Hōjin*) which is the reward for all the religious training undertaken before enlightenment and 3) The Body of Transformation (Skt. *Nirmanakāya*, J. *Ōjin*) which comes into being so that the Buddha may adapt himself to varying individualities and capacities. The Sōtō School emphasizes the most fundamental form of the Buddha which transcends this division: the historical Buddha who unites the three aspects in his own personality. He is termed in the Sōtō School "Daion Kyōshu Honshi Shākamuni Butsu Daioshō" which may be translated "The Great Benefactor, Founder of the Religion, Original Teacher, Shakyamuni Buddha, the Great Monk." Great Master Keizan said about him: "Even though He had the thirty-two marks of a Buddha, the good aspects and eighty appearances,

He always had the form and appearance of an old monk; His form was no different from our own." [*Zen is Eternal Life*, 1999, p. 225.] This old monk is beyond comparison and has a unique historical personality which cannot be duplicated. Great Master Dōgen strongly rejected the one-sided sectarian Buddhism which, ignoring the mainstream, clings to trivia and, straying from the main road, enters the side path. He taught a perfectly integrated Buddhism which existed before the division into Hinayāna or Mahāyāna. Accordingly, the object of veneration is Shakyamuni, the founder of the religion, who naturally predates any splits in dogma. The uninterrupted Transmission of the True Life starting from the Buddha is what we call "*Shoden no Buppō*" or "correctly transmitted Buddhism."

Now we must ask ourselves the question: How did the Buddha find the way to live in Truth? The answer has already been given above: through the practice of serene reflection meditation. Dōgen writes in "Bendōwa," a chapter of the *Shōbōgenzō*, "Shakyamuni, the Great Master, gave us this unequalled way to understanding and all the Buddhas of past, present and future were enlightened by means of Zazen in the same way as were also the Indian and Chinese Ancestors." [*Zen is Eternal Life*, 1999, pp. 181–182.] Thus, beginning with the historic Buddhas, all the Ancestors and Masters have experienced enlightenment by practicing meditation. At the time of his enlightenment, the Buddha is said to have declared, "*I was, am and will be enlightened* instantaneously *with* the universe." [*Zen is Eternal Life*, 1999, p. 224.] All sentient beings throughout the universe are enlightened by and with the enlightenment of the Buddha.

Although the Buddha was raised in luxury and later tried practicing asceticism, he discovered that true practice was the middle way. There is absolutely no need for us to practice asceticism, attempting to imitate the Buddha. Dōgen said in his "Gakudo Yōjinshū": "One who would train in Buddhism must first believe completely therein and, in order to do so, one must believe that one has already found the Way, never having been lost, deluded, upside down, increasing, decreasing or mistaken in the first place." [*Zen is Eternal Life*, 1999, pp. 177–178.] In essence this is to believe what the Buddha said at the time of his enlightenment: "*I was, am and will be enlightened* instantaneously *with* the universe." We are already on the path to enlightenment and are filled with the wisdom of the Buddha. Great Master Bodhidharma, the First Ancestor of Chinese Zen, said, "We deeply believe in accordance with the teachings of our Master that all mankind is endowed with an identical Buddha Nature." Our True Nature can be revealed only when we have thoroughly understood the doctrine of non-existence of the ego. Man's sacred nature is what we call the Buddha Mind or Buddha Nature. Great Master Bodhidharma taught us to believe that all mankind is inherently endowed with this nature. In the Sōtō School this nature is named *honshō no anjin*, i.e., the peaceful mind of original (inherent) enlightenment. Since we are in a state of enlightenment from the outset, serene reflection meditation cannot be regarded as a means to achieve enlightenment.

The *Shōbōgenzō*, written by Great Master Dōgen, is a virtual treasury of ideas about meditation. According to it, serene reflection meditation is not a way leading to enlightenment, but a religious practice carried on in a state of enlightenment. This Zazen differs from the meditation practiced by the Buddha before his enlightenment. It corresponds rather to the *jijuyū zammai* (meditation which is enjoyed by oneself) practiced after the enlightenment of the Buddha. This is a kind of meditation in which one fully experiences the bliss of enlightenment by oneself. Meditation itself, we may say, is Buddhahood. As meditation is the practice of the Buddha, those who engage in this practice are Buddhas. Serene reflection meditation which is based upon the peaceful state of mind that arises from original enlightenment is also termed "Wonderful Training." We view this "Wonderful Training" and enlightenment as one and the same thing, declaring: "Training and enlightenment are one."

Dōgen says of this in "Bendōwa," "It is heretical to believe that training and enlightenment are separable for, in

Buddhism, the two are one and the same. Since training embraces enlightenment, the very <u>beginning</u> of training contains the <u>whole</u> of original enlightenment; as this is so, the teacher tells his disciples never to search for enlightenment outside of training since the latter mirrors enlightenment." [*Zen is Eternal Life*, 1999, p. 186.] This is what we describe as the identity between original enlightenment and wonderful training. Although we do not deny the existence of training and enlightenment, we say that one must not cling to these concepts. This non-attachment we call untainted enlightenment and training. It is correctly transmitted Buddhism and is characterized by the harmony, not opposition, of enlightenment and training. Some may ask, "Since enlightenment and training are one, isn't the practice of meditation superfluous?" To this we must clearly answer, "No." It is easy to fall into such erroneous thinking about practicing meditation. Dōgen writes in his *Shōbōgenzō Zuimonki*, "My idea of the untainted man of religion is the person who gives himself completely to Buddhism and leads a religious life without troubling himself about the attainment of enlightenment." If we devote ourselves wholeheartedly to Buddhism without any desire to reach enlightenment, we become a living embodiment of Buddhism. Because Shinran, the founder of the Shin School of Buddhism, placed such emphasis on the reality of mankind, he was able to say, "Become a plain man!" Because Dōgen placed stress on the True Nature of man, he was able to say, "Become a Buddha!" We must incessantly practice serene reflection meditation and come to see that we are not "The Buddha," but there is nothing in us that is separate or apart from the Original Buddha. The ability to see our own shortcomings and errors is termed "confession and contrition." Although we feel that any breakage of the Precepts is a loathsome thing, we may say that there is nothing quite so beautiful as a former error which is repented. This urge to honestly look at one's shortcomings first arises as a result of deep faith.*

Serene reflection meditation is the basic expression of a religion which emphasizes training. Once its foundation is firmly laid, it may become an activity of the Buddha adaptable to our daily life. Since it is a practice which rests on enlightenment, it will transform our ordinary daily activities into sacred ones and reveal the peaceful mind of original enlightenment. After Great Master Dōgen arrived in Ningpo, he lived for a while in the boat which had brought him from Japan. One day the chief cook from a temple on Mt. Ayuwan (J. Aikuō) came

---

* The word "sange" which is translated as contrition and confession can be translated as "casting flower petals before the Buddha." It is quite different from accusing one's self of having sinned and holding on to guilt. It entails embracing and accepting responsibility for all one's past behavior and offering up the resultant suffering to the Unborn.

to the boat to buy some Japanese mushrooms. Dōgen invited him for a cup of tea and asked many questions about how Buddhism was practiced in China. Then becoming more personal, Dōgen asked him to stay longer; the chief cook replied: "I am afraid that is impossible for, should I stay longer, who will do to-morrow's cooking?" "Surely in a temple as big as Ayuwan-shan someone else is capable of cooking food? I cannot believe that the absence of one Chief Cook could cause trouble," Dōgen said. "Although I am old, I, as the Chief Cook, am in charge of cooking. Since this is the training of my old age how is it possible for me to give such duties to others? It must also be remembered that I did not get permission to stay out for the night," was his reply. "Surely it would be better for you to do Zazen or study kōans," Dōgen said. "Whatever is the use of working so hard merely at the duties of a Chief Cook?" He laughed heartily when hearing Dōgen's comment saying, "My good foreigner, you have no idea of the true meaning of Buddhist training, nor of its character." [*Zen is Eternal Life*, 1999, pp. 152–153.] Dōgen felt deeply ashamed and realized that his thinking had been erroneous. Because of the words of the old cook, for the first time he came to know the meaning of Buddhist training.

Religion is not something confined to the church or monastery. Nor is it limited to invoking the name of the Buddha or doing meditation. It must be revealed in the work we are doing at present. When we assume that each action undertaken in our daily life rests on a basis of original enlightenment, each act is in itself the act of a Buddha. The Fourth Ancestor, Tao-hsin (J. Daii Dōshin), and the Fifth Ancestor, Hung-jen (J. Daiman Kōnin), each had assemblies of more than five hundred monks. Since they did not receive any aid from the government, the necessary work for the maintenance of the monastery had to be divided among the monks: some doing the cooking, others the farming and the sweeping. The value of this work was held to be fully equal to that of formal seated meditation. Any work which is based upon the Buddha Nature is said to be radiant. All words and actions which emanate from religious training are a concrete expression of our faith and gratitude. The *Gyōji-no-Maki* by Dōgen says, "One's daily actions express one's gratitude for the great benevolence of the Ancestors." Each day, too, is sacred and can never come again. Takeko Kujō wrote in a poem, "Do you not see that the flower which scatters on the morn, so long as it has strength, will bloom?" Who can be sure of their life tomorrow? We must therefore seek the Way without hesitation and help others as much as possible as long as we are alive. Great Master Pai-chang (J. Hyakujō), even in his old age, continued to sweep the garden every morning along with his young disciples. One day his disciples, unable to bear the sight of their old master doing physical work, hid the broom. Hyakujō responded by saying, "If I do not work one day, I shall not eat that day," and declined all food.

At the end of the *Shushōgi* by Dōgen, it is written: "The life of this one day, to-day, is absolutely vital life; your body is deeply significant. Both your life and your body deserve love and respect for it is by their agency that Truth is practised and the Buddha's power exhibited: the seed of all Buddhist activity, and of all Buddhahood, is the true practice of Preceptual Truth." [*Zen is Eternal Life*, 1999, p. 103.] Our attitude toward life must radiate true Buddhism nourished at the very core of our being. Ultimately this will bear fruit for the benefit of both ourselves and others. This is what the peaceful mind of original enlightenment leads to. "[O]ur daily life should be spent constantly in selfless activity with no waste of time whatsoever." [*Zen is Eternal Life*, 1999, p. 103.]

In brief, the Sōtō School takes refuge in the historical Buddha existing before the division of his nature into three parts by later generations. His meditation is a pure act which, so long as it rests on a realization of original enlightenment, does not actively seek enlightenment externally. His everyday life is permeated by an uninterrupted expression of gratitude. These three points are the content of correct faith. Thus every act becomes Truth itself, every day a good day. The essential ideas of the Sōtō School may be summed up as follows: Shakyamuni

Buddha is the source from which our ideals are derived, his Life transmitted through an unbroken line of Ancestors becomes our Life; serene reflection meditation in which training and enlightenment are one is our fundamental religious practice. Our daily life is strengthened by the peaceful mind which arises from this practice; our religious training is continual; training and understanding deepen simultaneously and emphasis is placed upon expression of our gratitude toward the Buddha and Ancestors through selfless activity.

8.

Zen Buddhism and the West

The extent of western interest in Zen can be seen from the fact that when Buddhism is mentioned, almost immediately Westerners call Zen to mind. As Pure Land Buddhism bears a close external resemblance to Christianity, Westerners feel little attraction to it. Zen is most representative of the Orient. The simple yet profound culture which it created has great appeal to the West. Naturally, to communicate this to the West, it is absolutely necessary to have material written in European languages. In this respect the work of the late Dr. Daisetz Suzuki has been phenomenal. Likewise the aid of his late wife, Beatrice Suzuki, must not be overlooked. Many of his works in English have been translated into German and French, thus making their contents more available to a larger number of people. His most popularly read works are *An Introduction to Zen Buddhism, Living by Zen, Manual of Zen Buddhism, The Training of the Zen Buddhist Monk* and *Zen and Its Influence on Japanese Culture.* His practice and writings mainly belong to that of the Rinzai School, the other schools being almost completely ignored. When Western scholars refer to Zen, it is mainly that of Dr. Suzuki's variety. But is this really a good thing? The deep philosophy of Great Master Dōgen and original Zen of the Sōtō School have hardly been introduced at all. This certainly is a shortcoming. Western intellectuals are anxious to learn the difference between Rinzai Zen and Sōtō Zen. Professor Callway, who teaches Comparative Religion at Southwestern University, has undertaken this study and sent questions to scholars in Japan regarding this.

Friedrich Heiler, formerly professor of theology at Marburg University in Germany, excited considerable interest in Zen Buddhism with his "Buddhistische Versenkung" ("Buddhist Meditation"). According to Professor Dumoulin of Sophia University in Tokyo, Professor Heiler is enjoying good health despite his age. The former translated the *Wu-wen-kuan* (J. *Mumonkan*, a collection of kōans) into German and wrote a *History of the Zen Sect After the Sixth Patriarch* which was translated from the German into English by Mrs. Ruth Fuller Sasaki and published in a splendid format. Mrs. Sasaki maintains a Zen Institute in New York known as the Sōkei-an which aims chiefly at the dissemination of Zen among Americans. She is at present practising Zen in Kyōto. Father Naberfeld, who is a friend of Professor Dumoulin and who has a church in Kichijōji in Tokyo, has translated both the *Yuima Kyō* and *Shushōgi* into German. Dr. Nukariya Kaiten, former president of Komazawa University (a Sōtō Zen university in

Tokyo), published *The Religion of the Samurai* many years ago, expounding Sōtō Zen for the first time in English. Mr. Christmas Humphreys, (former) President of the London Buddhist Society, wrote a book on Zen called *Zen Buddhism*. However, his understanding of Sōtō Zen leaves much to be desired. He also authored a pamphlet known as the *Twelve Principles of Buddhism*, in which it may be said he was successful in epitomizing the essence of Buddhism. However, Pure Land ideas are not fully expressed in this.

Professor Alan Watts of the Asia Institute in San Francisco wrote *The Spirit of Zen Buddhism* and a smaller book simply titled *Zen* which generally follows the lines of Dr. Suzuki's Zen. In *Philosophy East and West*, a publication of the University of Hawaii, articles on Zen often appear. Several years ago an interesting exchange of articles took place between Dr. Suzuki and Professor Hu Shih, a Chinese scholar now at Princeton University. Professor Hu was formerly President of Peking University and for a time was the Chinese ambassador to the United States. He is an expert on the documents unearthed at Tun-huang (J. Tonkō) concerning Zen. His theories, which have exerted considerable influence on Japanese scholars, contain some rather extravagant statements. However, on the whole they are certainly deserving of serious notice. Nyogen Senzaki, a disciple of Sōen, is teaching Zen to Americans in Los Angeles. He has been active in the United

States for some fifty years and recently published a book titled *Zen*, in which may be found a free translation of Dōgen's "Rules for Meditation" (J. "Fukanzazengi"). At present he is working on an English translation of the *Mumonkan*.

Several years ago, *A Buddhist Bible*, edited by Dwight Goddard, was published in America. Saihō Lowe of Los Angeles who collaborated in this undertaking came to Japan. Despite his age, he has a deep interest in Buddhism and is an ordained Buddhist priest. Furthermore, Robert Stuart Clifton, Ven. Sumangalo, also a Buddhist priest, is very active in teaching Americans. Both men are Sōtō priests. The Rev. Clifton visited Japan this year and is now in Laos where he was again ordained.

Mr. John Blofeld, an Englishman, translated *The Path to Sudden Attainment* by Ta-chu Hui-hai (J. Daishu Ekai). The London Buddhist Society undertook its publication in 1948. *Zen*, a book in German written by Ohazama-Faust, was published many years ago. It contains a translation of the "Shōdō-ka" or "Song of Enlightenment." A former president of Komazawa University, Tachibana Shundō, who died this year at the age of 79, was an expert Pali scholar. While at Oxford he wrote *The Ethics of Buddhism* which the University Press published. This book contains many references to Zen. In recent years the Sōtō Church has published several works on Zen in English, including *What Is Zen?* and two pamphlets entitled *Zen*

Culture. Three different translations into English of Dōgen's *Shushōgi* have already been made. Recently, Mr. Ryūsaku Tsunoda, a lecturer on the history of Japanese religion at Columbia University, came to Japan. Mr. Tsunoda has a deep interest in Zen and has already translated Dōgen's *Shōbōgenzō Zuimonki* into English. A large part of the *Zuimonki* has already been translated into German by Mr. Hidemasa Iwamoto. The publication of articles on Buddhism in *Life* and *Time* magazines has aroused considerable interest throughout the world. In the February 14th issue of *Time,* an article about Dr. Jung of Switzerland drew much attention. Dr. Jung, a world-famous psychoanalyst, has a deep understanding of Zen. He wrote an introduction to the German edition of Dr. Suzuki's *Introduction to Zen Buddhism.* Dr. Jung, dissatisfied with Freud's psychoanalysis which sees sex at the root of all problems, struck out a new departure in psychology. He divides the mind into consciousness and unconsciousness and the latter further into individual and collective unconsciousness. Collective unconsciousness exists on three levels: firstly, for man it is "Anima" and woman "Animus;" secondly, for man "the old wise man," for woman "the earth mother;" and thirdly, for man and woman alike there is Self. This Self transcends the individual. In Zen this is called one's Original Face or the Old Master Within the House (J. *Okuri no Shujin-ō*) and indicates the Buddha Nature in people. To experience this fully is to be enlightened. This is what Jung calls "individuation." It is becoming Truth itself, a goal mankind is always trying to reach. In Zen we say "Show your original face." This showing of the "original face" is Jung's individuation. In his preface to Suzuki's *Introduction to Zen Buddhism,* Jung writes, "Zen is one of the most splendid manifestations of the Chinese spirit blossoming from the great and universal thought of the Buddhist world."

The kernel of Jung's psychoanalysis is difficult for most Westerners to grasp. This is because he has opened up a new field in Western thinking: he does not take the purely intellectual approach resorted to by his predecessors, but has shifted the emphasis to life itself as an integrated whole. Therefore, to an Oriental, particularly to one who has studied Zen, his ideas are easy to grasp. Westerners do not readily understand the paradoxical expressions of Zen. There are many paradoxes in religion. In terms of logic generally employed by people, it is impossible to express a thing exactly. A deep experience can only be expressed by paradox. In the *Gospel of St. Matthew* it says: "He that findeth his life shall lose it, and he that loseth his life for My sake shall find it." In Zen such paradoxes are very common indeed. "In the midst of nothing, an inexhaustible store is found," "First the great death, and then the great life," "Even though you fall from a towering cliff, you will be restored to life after your death," "Although you may have been separated from the Buddha for ages eternal, you have not left for a minute; although you face him all day, you have not faced him for a moment," "If you discard the Wonderful Practice, you are filled with the Original Enlightenment. When you shed off the Original Enlightenment, the Wonderful Practice is performed throughout your entire body" and other such phrases are innumerable. Such paradoxes force the person for whom they are intended to realize the limitations of logic and to find a way out of the impasse. In terms of existentialism, mankind is driven to a certain boundary (Ger. *Grenzsituation*) and then breaks through it to find his Real Self. According to the April 18th issue of *Time*, an artist named Ray did an abstract portrait of Dr. Suzuki which was later exhibited in the Willard Gallery. When Dr. Suzuki visited the gallery to view his portrait, Ray asked him, "Do you understand it?" Dr. Suzuki replied in the negative, whereupon Ray remarked, "When you say you don't know, then you know." This is really a paradox! Experience is the instantaneous grasping of things inwardly in their entirety. We cannot explain that which is not experienced. Experience means knowing things directly. Religion is the way to live by freeing oneself from ego. Such experience can never be expressed in logic. The most suitable way of expression is the paradox which transcends all contradictions. Jung says: "The spiritual concept necessary for Zen cannot be found in the West because Zen and its method of cultivation can exist only on the foundation of Buddhist culture." This view is certainly correct.

Zen indeed can only flourish on a foundation of Buddhist culture. Therefore, to understand Zen, it is necessary to know Buddhism and Buddhist culture first.

In America, interest in Buddhism is highly developed. An Oriental approach to life is sought to offset the mechanical civilization. The Second World War brought East and West into closer contact with each other. Furthermore, authorities in all fields of culture and science under pressure of the war took up residence in the United States. Lectures on Buddhism are given in many theological schools. In addition Yale, Columbia, Harvard, Chicago, Stanford, California and other universities have lectures on Indian Philosophy, Buddhism and Zen. Professor Hamilton of Union Theological Seminary has done much research in Yuishiki Buddhist Philosophy. Professor A. K. Reischauer's *Studies in Japanese Buddhism* is a well-known work. His son, Edwin Reischauer, is Professor of Japanese language and culture at Harvard and recently finished a translation of *Ennin's Travels in China*. Professor Elisseeff of Harvard studied for many years in Japan and speaks fluent Japanese. (He together with Dr. Warner deserve great praise for having saved Kyōto from air raids during the War.) Professor Rahder of Yale University, a veritable genius in language, formerly taught at Leyden University in the Netherlands. He published the Sanskrit text of the *Daśabhūmi Sūtra* (J. *Jūji Kyō*) with translations in other languages. At present he is engaged in a study of the *Kuang-hung-ming Chi* (J. *Kōgumyō Shū*). Professor Edgerton of Yale University published a *Buddhist Hybrid Sanskrit Grammar and Dictionary*. Professor Lessing, a German scholar, who is now at the University of California, is an acknowledged authority on Tibet. Professor Edgerton also gave a series of lectures at the University of California on the Tower of Asoka and Buddhist Sanskrit. Japanese studies are most advanced at the University of Michigan. Professor Frank Huntley of the English Department received actual training in Zen. Professor Morris of the University of Chicago values Buddhism for its tolerant spirit which shows a way of life for the future. Professor Babbit, formerly of Harvard, translated the *Dharmapada Sūtra* into English, and in an essay entitled "Buddha and the Orient" included at the end of his translation, he urges all Americans to pay attention to Buddhism. Lectures in Oriental languages are also given at Pennsylvania, Johns Hopkins, North Carolina and other universities. In universities in England, France and Germany, Sanskrit, Pali and Tibetan are taught. Because of limitations of space we will omit mention of them here. Every tradition of Mahāyāna Buddhism has been introduced into the United States from Japan. However, second and third generation Japanese-Americans are desirous of English language religious services. We are eagerly looking forward to the appearance of young people who have firm faith in their religion and sound linguistic ability.

The Essentials of Buddhist Philosophy by the late Dr. Takakusu was the text for a series of lectures he gave at Hawaii University. The book is very useful, but unfortunately the section on Zen is incomplete. Mr. Petzold's *On Buddhist Meditation*, published by the Asiatic Society, largely concerns Tendai meditation, but its references to the meditation of Zen are most interesting. Recently, Professor Burtt compiled a book entitled *The Teachings of the Compassionate Buddha* to which he added his own comments. Although much space is devoted to the Pure Land Teaching, also included are the "no-mind" of Zen, the sudden enlightenment of Shen-hui (J. Shin'e), the kōan of Nan-ch'üan (J. Nansen), etc. There is much else worthy of mention in regard to studies on Zen in the West, but unfortunately it cannot be explored here because of limitations of space. [This chapter has information that was current in 1960. A great deal has changed in the last half of the twentieth century with Buddhist teachings and practice in the West, but the chapter is included here for historical reference. Editor's note.]

9.

The Religion of the Future

What will be the nature of the religion of the future? This is indeed a big problem. We may say that religion is essentially divisible into subjective and objective aspects. By the subjective aspect we mean the religious experience of the founder and the spirit of this which lives on in the religion of his followers, transcending the limitations of time and place. The objective aspect is the objectively materialized content of the founder's experience and includes doctrine, credo and system. It is only natural that the objective aspect of religion is conditioned by time and place. However, as a result of idealizing its founder and emphasizing its completeness, it tends to become retrogressive. In order to free religion from this stagnation, it becomes necessary to introduce reforms continuously. However, since religion has both subjective and objective aspects, one can mediate for the other. The development of the objective side of religion deepens the substantial subjective content as well as the objective side. The basic mission of religion is fulfilled when these two sides complement each other.

How does the objective aspect of religion, i.e., the doctrine, credo and system, develop? Development must mean a steady increase in values. The factors which stimulate the development of religion are: 1) an interchange of different cultures, 2) the development of scientific culture, 3) an advance in moral concepts and 4) changes in social structure. Of course religion belongs to that realm which transcends the narrow confines of science, morality, culture and society. But if it is to develop in the future as a cultural religion, it cannot overlook the factors mentioned above.

The impact of the effect of different cultures on religion is very great. The Crusades from a religious point of view may have had certain shortcomings, but their merit in introducing Eastern culture to the West and Western culture to the East is certainly undeniable. The case of the Second World War is similar: on the one hand it was a great tragedy, but on the other, it was responsible for bringing about a great cultural interchange between East and West. Needless to say, we earnestly desire this interchange, but without the curse of war. Developments in transportation facilities will do much toward the realization of this goal. In particular, achievements in the field of aeronautics have contributed much toward reducing the isolation of countries throughout the world. After the end of the Second World War, representative groups of people from all walks of life in Japan visited the United States to observe the religious, cultural and educational facilities. This exerted a considerable influence on Japanese religion. Religion is a cultural phenomenon. Therefore the interchange of different cultures will contribute much to the development of religion.

The impetus given to religious development by the advancement of science and culture must never be overlooked. Religion concerns itself primarily with a world transcending science. Religion cannot for that reason, however, oppose science. The more primitive the religion, the more numerous will its superstitious elements be. It is very infantile to say that there can be no religion without belief in miracles and supernatural powers. Religion which cannot embrace science will not be able to lead the future culture. Religion can only be purified when it is freed from superstitious elements. However, no matter how much science may advance, religion can never be replaced by it, because it covers ground that is completely alien to science. Religion must lean more on science, but so long as it cannot free itself from unscientific ideas, it will not be able to carry out its mission. The evolution of science and culture will surely stimulate the growth of religion and will transform and purify it.

The elevation of moral concepts is also a very important factor in the development of religion. Morality is the set of social rules which men must follow. It is manifested by desiring good, accumulating virtue and fulfilling one's duty. In Japan at present, social morality is considered more important than the former feudal morality, which was concerned essentially with the relationship between lord and vassal. Under democracy we must all help each other and seek peace and happiness. Individual morality is of course important, but social morality is even more important because the individual cannot live apart from society. The development of religion is accelerated by the elevation of moral ideals. Accordingly, we may say that the more highly religion is developed, the greater the number of moral elements it will contain.

It is an undeniable fact that changes in social structure stimulate the development of religion. It is said that society progresses from feudalism to capitalism and then to socialism. Of course, there are many problems concerning order, value and other points in this development, but it clearly shows that man is always looking forward to the realization of an ideal society. The ideal society which Buddhism seeks is a world filled with compassion and justice. It is problematical whether in the final analysis this wish can be realized in the present world. However, great men of religion have already brought this about within themselves in the present world. Even if perfection of society is not possible, we should not abandon the ideal. Ancient religion reflects the social structure of the society in which it developed. Therefore, we cannot ignore the influence which alterations in the social structure exert on religion. Religion in feudal society is necessarily feudal, in democratic society it must be democratic. But in modern religion, feudal vestiges still remain fairly strong. We must gradually sweep these vestiges away and return to the true form of religion in which the subjective aspect, i.e., the religious experience of the founder himself, will again come to the fore. The fundamental principle in Luther's reformation can be summed up as "through faith alone." Faith and religious experience are indispensable to religion. With this we can revitalize the retrogressive objective aspect of religion. In any case, it cannot be denied that changes in social structure serve to stimulate development in religion. Religion is not something for a special group of people. It is found deep in the heart of all people. The world of religion does not discriminate against the dull in favor of the wise, nor does it draw distinctions between men and women, clergy and lay people. It must break the narrow confines of nationality and spread its doctrine throughout the world. Religion which makes no distinctions between the worldly and the unworldly will be a part of our daily life and will remain a strong, vital force in society. It is desirable that future religion should equally reject both the life which falls into complacency as well as the religious life of isolation from worldly things. It must criticize and transcend the false life, but at the same time return again to real life and enable it to be lived in truth.

The religion of the coming period must not contradict scientific truth. Science aims at both freeing itself from all preconceived ideas and the systematic classification of knowledge free from contradiction. Although religion belongs to a realm which transcends science, we cannot say that it contradicts it. Miracles and supernatural power are not necessary accessories of religion. The culture of the future must include science and have as its basis a religious spirit which will serve as its guide.

This religion must stand upon a firm philosophical base. Philosophy is nothing other than the most fundamental realization of historical actuality. The object of philosophy is the search for the way to live in truth through logic. Philosophy must not become a lady-in-waiting for theology as happened in the Middle Ages. However, religious doctrine which has no philosophical background is both weak and shallow. Therefore, the religion of the coming period must not be opposed to science and will require a strong philosophical foundation.

Finally, in the new religion, gratitude and a desire for continuous progress must always supplement each other. In the religions of the past, one of these two elements was often lacking. Although the concept of gratitude may have existed, the desire for progress was missing. The reverse also was sometimes the case. We believe that gratitude and the effort to move forward complement each other like the two wheels of a cart. Those people who have realized the depths of their mistakes and shortcomings may view the Absolute transcendentally and, basking in the light of Its compassion, be filled with immeasurable joy. Those who feel impermanence deeply and live each moment in truth view the Absolute inwardly and, finding their Original Self, move forward boldly.

Even if future religion does not take an attitude of inward transcendentalism, the Absolute must be sought inwardly as one's own True Nature, which must always be free from selfish desire and egoism. In the religion of inward transcendentalism the bliss of religious Truth and concrete action complement each other, and while infinite ideals are being sought, self-liberation is obtained and the Original Self is thereby manifested. We believe that in such a religion, life can be given to morality, hope to mankind, ideals to politics and peace to the world. We feel convinced that Buddhism is just such a religion. Einstein said that the future religion will be a cosmic religion. This would transcend the concept of a personified God and would possess neither dogma nor theology. It would include both the natural world and the world of thought and would be based upon a religious feeling arising from the realization that all existence belongs to an integrated whole.

Einstein declared that Buddhism is a representative example. We believe that the religion of the two Ancestors, Great Masters Dōgen and Keizan, particularly fits this description because 1) its ideal is a perfectly integrated Buddhism free from sectarianism living in the spirit of Buddha, 2) it insisted on the equality of men and women long before the Renaissance when women in the West were still looked down upon, 3) it was a pioneer in the world of Japanese thought, teaching a deep philosophy which embraces a scientific outlook arrived at after deep thought and sharp logic and 4) it achieves a perfect balance between practice and understanding and is the correct way for living in truth and enabling others to do so, thereby expressing our gratitude in our everyday life. It is in this that we can find the historical significance of Buddhism leading up to the present time and in it a great suggestion as to the religion of the future.

APPENDIX I*

WESTERN INTEREST IN BUDDHIST MEDITATION

a.   *Reasons for Western Interest in Buddhist Meditation*

F or man, the most important thing is life. Life is always changing, flowing, and it is the matrix from which new life is created. Anything without life is dead. Life has creativity and vitality as its essential elements. Originally, all living things embodied creativity and vitality. But eventually, over many years, they become rigid, form-ridden and dogmatic. In *Decline of the West* Oswald Spengler (1880–1936) wrote that the West has civilization but no culture. This weakness has now become apparent in politics, economics and science.

Many taboos have emerged in social convention and traditions. Techniques and machines brought about the industrial revolution; man has been taken up into the cogs of machinery

---

* Some of the information here seems only a summary of previous chapters, but there is also additional material.

and has lost his basic humanity. Man, surrounded by machines, mass communication and organized systems, has become alienated from freedom and spontaneity. Buddhist religious practice based in meditation seems unusually well-suited to break the deadlock facing modern man. Science has now emerged into the atomic age and entered the space age. Originally based on humanism, science gradually came to be considered all-powerful and autonomous from religion and humanity.

In this way, it moved in the wrong direction, luring mankind toward destruction. Buddhist meditation seems to have a vital role in correcting this false tendency of science. Although the world is said to be moving toward a thaw, the two ideological camps are still in sharp conflict. The Third World nations are caught in the middle, wavering from left to right. Buddhism offers the possibility of basically undercutting this dualism. It can help man overcome the conflict of ideologies for the first time. The West tends to emphasize the individual over the group. But even in individual man, there are two facets. They are the false self and the True Self. No matter how much the individual is emphasized, it does no good if the emphasis is on the false self. Through the True Self the dignity of man emerges. In Christianity, God is worshiped as "an absolute other." He is separated from man. Zen, on the other hand, returns man to this original wholeness and shows him his True Self. In Buddhism, the True Self is called Buddha Nature.

Buddha Nature includes man's religious nature and true humanity. It is deeply involved in human dignity. Thinkers in Europe and America have sensed this. Zen, with its emphasis on one's True Self, has given them new insights into human potentiality. Christianity talks about a future kingdom of heaven and makes it the dwelling place of the soul. But Zen considers this too far removed from the actual world.

The practice of Zen helps man live fully in this world. This is called the expression of full function. It stresses the present rather than future, this place rather than heaven. It aims at making the Pure Land come alive in the present moment. In religion the most important thing is not miracles or the supernatural. Religion of course transcends the world of science, but it should not conflict with science.

Any religion that hopes to appeal to modern man must embrace science as well as transcend it. Zen does this. In conclusion, the practice of Zen: 1) frees man from enslavement to machines and re-establishes his humanity, 2) eases mental tension and brings peace of mind and 3) enables man to use his full potentialities in daily life. From these grow the characteristics of simplicity, profundity and vitality that have attracted so many Westerners to Zen Buddhism.

b. Zen in the West

Zen penetrates into man's True Self and helps him manifest It in daily life. In the past few years Zen has enjoyed something of a boom among many intellectuals in Europe and America. This stems partly from its capacity to break the intellectual deadlock induced by mechanical civilization, to correct one-sided dependence on science and to soften the conflict of ideologies.

In addition, the practice of Buddhist meditation responds to the modern need for simplicity, profundity, creativity and vitality. I would like to discuss Western Zen under six classifications: "beat" Zen, conceptual Zen, square Zen, Suzuki Zen, native Zen, and Zen.

Beat Zen—This is the Zen popular among the "beat" in America and the "angry young men" in England. Its proponents rebel against convention and tradition. Seeking freedom, they try to model their actions on those of the monks in Sung China. [Wildly independent monks such as ones depicted as tearing up the Scriptures. This has been twisted, from its original intent of pointing to the transmission beyond the Scriptures, to disrespect for authority. Editor's note.] But most of them lack creativity and moderation. They represent, however, a phase of the process toward deeper understanding.

106

Conceptual Zen—This is the Zen derived from reading many books. It tries to grasp Zen conceptually and fails because Zen is a practice and not a concept. But the concept can serve as a starting point.

Square Zen—This is the Zen bound by rigid forms and rituals. Its advocates put weight on solving *kōans* and receiving the certification of the Zen masters. But since Zen stresses vital freedom, there is no need to be so strictly enslaved by form.

Suzuki Zen—This is the Zen grown through the works of Professor Daisetz Suzuki. His contributions to Western understanding of Zen have been tremendous, but his Zen tends to emphasize enlightenment through the *kōan*. If this emphasis is too strong, Zen loses its original "abrupt" flavor and becomes step-like.

Native Zen—This is the Zen based on native philosophic tradition. It is represented, for example, by the writing of Professor Van Meter Ames of Cincinnati University. It resembles the *kakugi* (syncretism) method of early China, which adapted Buddhist thought to the native heritage. This method contributed much to the development of Mahāyāna Buddhism in China. This type of Western Zen has potential for contributing significantly to Zen in Europe and America.

Zen, or Serene Reflection Meditation—This is the Zen that grows from right training. Here the works of Great Master Dōgen, the founder of the Serene Reflection Meditation School in Japan, offer many pointers, especially in his explanation of the identity of original enlightenment and thorough training. The Serene Reflection Meditation Tradition grows out of a deep philosophic background, understanding of the historical development of Buddhism based on the Precepts and requiring the guidance of a true Zen master. From these will come an authentic Transmission. But, of course, this Transmission should be creative; the disciple should not cling to the teachings of his master, but should transcend them. This is the meditation practice described at the end of the *Scripture of Great Wisdom:* "going, going, going on beyond and always going on beyond,—always BECOMING Buddha. Hail! Hail! Hail!"*

---

* *The Liturgy of the Order of Buddhist Contemplatives for the Laity,* comp. Rev. Master P.T.N.H. Jiyu-Kennett, M.O.B.C., 2nd ed. rev. (Mt. Shasta, California: Shasta Abbey Press, 1990), p. 74.

c. Characteristics of Zen and its Art

To study true Zen, Westerners should ideally visit Japan. This is because monasteries still flourish in Japan under the guidance of Zen masters. There are also some fine scholars of Zen thought and historical background. Probably, one year of intensive Zen training in Japan equals three years of study in the West.

In Japan, Zen is divided into three schools: Rinzai, Sōtō and Ōbaku. The Rinzai School has many branches, each with a head temple; the most famous of these are probably Engaku-ji Temple at Kamakura and Myōshin-ji Temple in Kyōto. The leading Sōtō Temples are Eihei-ji Temple in Fukui Prefecture and Sōji-ji Temple in Yokohama. The head temple of the Ōbaku School is Manpuku-ji Temple in the suburbs of Kyōto. The monasteries belonging to these Zen schools facilitate the practice of Zen. The Rinzai teaching was brought from China by Eisai, and it had great influence among the warrior class during the Kamakura period. Rinzai Zen emphasizes enlightenment through the *kōan*. It is characterized by severity of discipline and by the use of shouts and blows. The Sōtō School arose from the teachings of Great Master Dōgen. It gained popularity among common people of Japan and became the largest of the Zen schools. Its major tenet is the identity of enlightenment and training. Sōtō Zen emphasizes thorough training, or the application of the meditation practice to the details of daily life. The Ōbaku School, founded by Ingen, linked up with the *nembutsu* of Ming China. It is the smallest Zen School today.

The general characteristics of the three meditation schools are as follows: 1) training in meditation, 2) finding the True Self, or the direct experience of the Unborn, 3) vitalizing this training and understanding in daily life, 4) not clinging to the literal meaning of the Scriptures, but learning to act in accordance with their spirit, 5) transmitting the Truth from heart to heart. Since coming to Japan, Zen has had vital influence on architecture, sculpture, painting, calligraphy, gardening, flower arrangement, *yōkyoku, noh, haiku* and the tea ceremony. It has produced a unique art. At its best, this art is characterized by simplicity, profundity, creativity and vitality. Simplicity includes economy of color and line and directness of style. The garden at Ryoan-ji Temple in Kyōto and the *sumie* drawings of Sesshū are typical examples. Profound depth is seen in the apparent simplicity of Zen art. Examples include the *haiku* of Bashō and the *noh* plays of Zeami. The creativity of Zen art is found in its closeness to life and its impulse toward fresh expression. This art uses form to transcend form. Professor E. Herrigel called this "to climb on the shoulders of his teacher." Sesshū's paintings and Ryōkan's calligraphy typify the creative art produced by the direct understanding of the

Truth from meditation. Vitality is evident in the vigor and free flow of this art. John Dewey's phrase "vital freedom" fittingly describes this characteristic. The painting and calligraphy of Hakuin and the asymmetrical bowls used in the tea ceremony are good examples. Simplicity, profundity, creativity and vitality characterize the spirit of the meditation and its practice. This may account for the great interest in Zen among many Westerners today.

THE GIST OF SŌTŌ ZEN

a. What is Serene Reflection Meditation?

The practice of Buddhist meditation and its influence on culture are unique to the East. But recently this practice has found admirers in the West, primarily through the writings of Dr. D. T. Suzuki. In America, Zen is currently enjoying something of a boom. In the West, Buddhism is sometimes even identified with Zen. Briefly, Zen first saw the light of day in India, developed on Chinese soil and reached its most mature expression in Japan. We can readily see why its outlook is so wide. Also, because Buddhist meditation has maintained an inseparable relationship with the culture of the countries in which it developed, its contents gradually became richer and deeper. Although the word "Zen" is of Indian origin, it has entered the vocabularies of most foreign languages. Zen is the Japanese pronunciation of the Chinese character pronounced *ch'an* in modern Chinese, which was chosen by the Chinese because of its phonetic approximation to the Prakrit *jhān. Jhān* is the shortened form of *jhāna*, in Sanskrit *dhyāna*, suffering the loss of the final vowel. *Dhyāna* means "to think." The meaning of *dhyāna* is usually represented in Buddhist texts by the word *jōryo*, "to think quietly," i.e., to think after freeing the mind from all distractions: serene reflection. The practice of *dhyāna* antedates Buddhism. The members of the highest of the four hereditary castes in India, the Brahman caste, devoted themselves to the practice of *dhyāna*.

Indian thinkers dwelt largely in forests in order to escape the intense heat. They would seat themselves in a specific posture beneath a large tree and meditate, regarding such meditation not merely as a religious task, but as a great pleasure. Such meditation came to be known as *just-sitting meditation (zazen)*, the characteristic meditation of the Zen School. It was held to be *"anraku no hōmon,"* i.e., "the comfortable way." Zen is not a theory. Religious truth is to be experienced through the practice of Zen, and this truth works in unity with practice. Only after Zen (*dhyāna* meditation) was adopted by Buddhists were its methods and goals sharply defined. Serene reflection meditation is basic to Buddhism because the enlightenment of its founder, Gautama Buddha, was achieved through this practice. The Buddha's meditation does not separate body and mind, nor does it seek rebirth in heaven after death. It is the essential method of gaining the ideal of perfecting the personality. Therefore, serene reflection meditation is considered the most fundamental religious exercise in Buddhism. A movement arose within Chinese Buddhism attempting to unify all of Buddhism through the practice of meditation. This movement is what we call the Zen School. The founder of the Zen School is Bodhidharma. He brought no sacred Scripture with him from India when he arrived in Canton, China about 470 C.E. He journeyed to North China, crossing the Yang-tze River and took up residence in the Shao-lin Temple on Sung-shan Mountain near Lo-yang, the then capital, and devoted himself to the practice of serene reflection meditation.

Bodhidharma's view of Buddhism, briefly stated, is that all beings possess the Buddha Nature (*Buddhata, Buddhatva*) i.e., have a nature identical with that of the Buddha, and through the practice of Zen they can come to realize this in its deepest sense. Realization of the Buddha Mind found within us is the essence of Buddhist meditation. When we realize this Buddha Mind inherent within us, it will be manifested in our everyday life and will serve as a means to help society in general and our fellow man in particular.

Some scholars say that Zen is non-subjective self-awakening, but I feel that it must be realized in daily activity through practicing serene reflection meditation; otherwise it will only be a dreamy concept.

Life magazine ran a special on Buddhism in its March 7, 1955 issue in which it took up the Zen School under the title, "An Austere Sect which Seeks Out Truth by Meditation and Intuition." Zen thought stands high among Mahāyāna schools, and its practice is firm like that of the Theravāda. Its gift to the

Orient, and particularly to Japan, has been great indeed. The characteristics of Zen culture are a simple form combined with a free and easy style. Western intellectuals and artists recently developed an appreciation of this simple and profound characteristic of Zen, which accounts for their growing interest in it. In brief then, Zen is a religion which aims at putting the heart at rest through the practice of meditation, allowing us to realize the full depth of the Buddha Mind inherent within us.

b. Development in Zen

Although the word "Zen" appears to have but one meaning, in reality it embraces many different forms. Tsung-mi (J. Shūmitsu) of the Tang Dynasty (618–907 C.E.) in China divided it into five groups: first, Non-Buddhist Zen (J. *Gedō-Zen*); second, popular Zen (J. *Bompu-Zen*); third, Hinayāna Zen (J. *Shōjō-Zen*); fourth, Mahāyāna Zen (J. *Daijō-Zen*); fifth, Zen of the Highest Vehicle (J. *Saijōjō-Zen*). Non-Buddhist Zen comprises the *dhyāna* (meditation) of Brahmanism, the Yoga Philosophy (one of the six schools of "unorthodox" philosophy in India), and non-Buddhist meditation in general like that of Ālāra Kalama and Udraka Rāmaputra. Popular Zen is an amateurish type of meditation practiced by Buddhists within the framework of Buddhism. "Hinayāna" means an abandoned or discarded vehicle and indicates a teaching which is no longer usable. Naturally those who belong to this school do not use this appellation because of its obvious bias, but call their school Theravāda, i.e., the Way of the Elders. Observance of the Precepts and practice of meditation constitute the essence of the Theravāda. Those who mainly practiced meditation were called yogins and were distinguished from those who emphasized scholarship. The former were particularly respected. Mahāyāna Zen is that form of Zen which is practiced by members of the

116

Mahāyāna traditions. Many of the Mahāyāna sūtras were preached by the Buddha after he entered samādhi (meditation, consequently Zen). For example, *Mahāprajñāpāramitā Sūtra* was preached while the Buddha was in the *Saurādhi Raja Samadhi*, *Avatamsaka Sūtra* in the *Sagaramudra Samādhi*, *Saddharma Pundarīka Sūtra* in the *Anata Nirdesa Pratisthana Samādhi*, *Mahāparinivāna Sūtra* in the *Acala Samādhi*. Therefore we might say that the whole of Mahāyāna Buddhism is the product of the meditation of the Buddha. Lastly, Tsung-mi lists the Zen of the Highest Vehicle, which is the understanding and practice of meditation transmitted by Bodhidharma. In the Meditation Schools, Scripture is not considered the final authority; these schools aim at the realization of the Buddha Heart (Buddha Nature) within us. It was in order to achieve this that Bodhidharma advocated the *practice* of meditation.

Of the first three Ancestors of the Zen School, following Bodhidharma, each had only one main disciple who succeeded him. They practiced the *dhūtas* (J. *zuda,* austere religious exercises), but exerted little influence on society in general. However, beginning with the fourth Ancestor, Tao-hsin (J. Dōshin) and the fifth Ancestor, Hung-jen (J. Kōnin), we find them having a large number of disciples, totaling perhaps five hundred or more, assembled on Mt. Shuang-feng (J. Sōbō) leading a collective life. Zen then changed from a largely Indian school to one which was more suited to Chinese ideals and began to exert influence over Chinese society. Work in these large Zen monasteries is divided among the monks; some do the cooking, some do the cleaning, others attend to farming, etc. Such work is designated *samu* (working meditation) in the Zen School. In the Serene Reflection School equal importance is attached both to *samu* and to purely religious matters.

If we probe deeply into our hearts, we shall arrive at our nature which is identical with that of Buddha. Since all things are based on the Buddha Mind, we might say all things have the same value as just-sitting meditation. It is for this reason that Zen has achieved such spiritual depth in China. Accordingly, no matter where we are or what work we do, we can always live in the meditative spirit. Once we have realized the essence of this spirit, we can free ourselves from a narrow interpretation of Scripture and look at it with detachment. We might say that we are no longer "turned" (controlled) by the Scripture, but "turn" (control) it ourselves. [The first Scripture given by the Buddha was termed "the turning of the wheel of the Law." Editor's note.]

It is evident that in order to lead a collective life, we must establish a certain set of rules which will govern our relations with each other. Such rules are called *shingi*. Since the Chinese have traditionally placed emphasis on ritual and ceremony, it is only likely that they would attach much importance to *shingi*. This also enabled Zen monks to establish their own independent monasteries. The center point of the Zen monasteries is the *zendō* or *sodō* (meditation hall or monks' hall) in which serene reflection meditation is practiced. There is also a *Hattō* or Lecture Hall where the Buddha Dharma is taught by Zen masters as representatives of the Buddhas and Ancestors.

The sixth Ancestor of the Zen School is known in history as Hui-neng (J. Enō). Through his efforts, Zen was finally turned into a thoroughly Chinese school capable of reaching the common people. Hui-neng had a great number of disciples, but among them two are outstanding: Nan-yüeh Huai-jang (J. Nangaku Ejō, 677–744) and Ch'ing-yuan Hsing-ssu (J. Seigen Gyōshi, ?–740). The two schools of Zen founded by Lin-chi (J. Rinzai) and Wei-yang (J. Igyō) belong to the school of Nan-yüeh, while the three schools Ts'ao-Tung (J. Sōtō), Yün-men (J. Ummon), and Fa-yen (J. Hōgen) stem from the Ch'ing-yuan line. These are collectively known as the Five Houses of Zen. Lin-chi is famous for his sharp wits and freedom of style. A sudden identity between master and disciple engaged in a serious exchange of questions and answers is characteristic of the Wei-yang School. Ts'ao-Tung aims at the harmonization of understanding and action by putting a strong emphasis on the manifestation of meditation in every activity (J. *gyōji*). It utilized the divination techniques[*] that flourished in the Tang Dynasty and taught the theory of the Five Ranks (C.*wuwei*, J.*goi*). The Yün-men School achieves the cessation of delusion by the use of unique dialogues, while the Fa-yen School eliminates illusion by using the Kegon doctrine. Although Zen itself aims at the realization of the wisdom that the Buddha Mind is inherent in all beings, it recognizes the individuality of the master and the many different ways of teaching the same truth. For this reason, Zen split into five different schools in China.

---

* This shows the influence of Taoism and Chinese culture on Buddhism and was not used in India nor has it been taken to Japan or America. Chinese Temples may still use divination. Chinese Buddhist priests are frequently embarrassed by it because any fortune telling is totally contrary to the direct experience of the Truth which is central to Buddhist practice. Reference to the *I Ching*, or Chinese *Book of Changes* can be found in the morning office of the Sōtō Zen temples in *The Most Excellent Mirror—Samādhi*.

c. What Are the Cultural Influences
of Zen?

Z en emphasizes practice rather than theory and devotes itself to bringing about liberation from life and death. It respects bold actions and admires the simple life. It follows, however, its rules of morality and etiquette, especially in regard to the manifestation of meditation in every activity. This outlook has penetrated deeply into the Oriental mind and exerted a great influence on its cultural expression. When the Meditation Schools of Buddhism were introduced into Japan, they were immediately adopted by the warrior class in their education and contributed much to the forging of the warrior spirit.* Toward the end of the Kamakura Period (1180–1333 C.E.) the practice of Buddhist meditation played a leading role in fostering education and culture and truly distinguished itself in the fields

---

* Buddhism emphasizes not killing and causing no harm to others. The Japanese culture had a strong warrior tradition and used Buddhism to make their warriors better fighters. This is a cultural distortion of Buddhist teaching, and is very likely to happen in whatever country Buddhism happens to go. The Chinese mixed Taoism and Confucianism with Buddhism. Americans developed Beat Zen and other distortions to avoid confronting the painful process of honestly looking at oneself.

of architecture, sculpture, painting, calligraphy, landscape gardening, *yōkyoku noh* (drama), *renga, haiku* (kinds of poetry) and tea ceremony and created what may aptly be termed a Zen culture. The characteristics of this culture, under the influence of Zen, are simplicity combined with strength and vital freedom which are at one with nature. The culture, thus influenced, when put into a mold will always break out of it and transcend it. The spirit of Buddhist meditation has penetrated every field of Japanese culture and art, and through its emphasis on simplicity and profundity it has made its value everlasting.

In Japan, architecture and sculpture influenced by Zen differ radically from those of other schools, not being addicted to bright colors. Materials are used in the natural form without adhering to any stylized pattern. All of this may be said to be the embodiment of the fundamental spirit of the meditation. The *Shari-den* hall of the Engaku-ji Temple in Kamakura is a representative work of this period. Typical of Zen paintings is the *suiboku-ga* style which is done in India ink. There are many very well-known Zen painters, and among them Sesshū (1420–1506 C.E.) is possibly the most famous. His view as to the relation between Zen and art is significant: "Painting and Zen are one (*gazen' ichimi*)." His *haboku* landscapes are fine models of masculinity and strength and have an inseparable kinship with nature itself. His portraits which consist largely of just head and shoulders also represent a highly developed form of Zen art.

Calligraphy is another field of art in which Zen priests have made a lasting name for themselves. Sesson, Chūhō, Gukyoku, Mokuan, Sokuhi and others are known to all lovers of calligraphy in Japan. The appreciation of such calligraphy more than any other form of art represents the beauty of line.

The ultimate ideal in Japanese landscape gardening is the elimination of all trace of artificiality and the embodiment of nature as it is. Such temples as the Myōgetsuin of Kamakura, Daitoku-ji, Tenryū-ji and Ryōan-ji of Kyōto have superb gardens which have long been popular with the Japanese. Among these are not a few which were created by Zen priests. Such gardens often include mountains which produce elegance by bringing both the near and far into play.

In literature *yōkyoku* are the texts used in the *noh* drama. Their essence is in a representation of the serene world of dream and phantasms. The texts are concise and abound in scriptural reference to Buddhist texts which have their true meaning outside the narrow confines of the word itself. *Renga* poetry, which was very popular during the Ashikaga period, contains a certain harmony which because of its popular composition can be understood by the masses. Experts believe that the essence of poetry is well expressed in the Buddhist phrase

descriptive of Gautama Buddha: *Mushi dokugo*, i.e., enlightenment accomplished by oneself without relying upon a teacher.*
In the poem a harmony is achieved between opposites, and it
may be viewed as a direct attestation of sudden enlightenment.
Along with the *renga* described above, are the *haiku* which are
similar in content. The profound *haiku* produced by the master
Bashō (1644–1694 C.E.) are quite unintelligible without understanding the meditation practice which produced them. In a
brief passing moment the true form of all things can be seen.
Such is *haiku*, poetry influenced by the meditation practice of
the poet. In summary, the ultimate goal of the artist is to be
enlightened by himself, to have his work express his religious
understanding spontaneously.

Tea was introduced into Japan in 1214 C.E. and at first
was used chiefly as a medicine. The tea ceremony was begun by
Murata Shukō (1421–1502 C.E.), and reached its zenith with the
master Sen-no-Rikyū (1522–1591 C.E.). The influence of Zen
on the four principles of the tea ceremony—harmony, respect,
purity and serenity—is obvious at first glance. The etiquette of
the classic tea room owes a great deal to the spiritual
ceremonies of Buddhism in their skillful combination of the
simple with the profound. The founder of *Setoyaki* pottery,
Katō Kagemasa, journeyed to China in the company of Great

---

* See footnote p. 41.

Master Dōgen, the founder of the Japanese Sōtō School, and there, under the influence of Buddhist practice, grasped the essence of pottery craftsmanship and art. Much of the Japanese pottery now enjoying favor in the United States is produced in Seto.

The practice of serene reflection meditation, which has an inseparable connection with the Japanese term *mono no aware* (the ah! ness of things), has produced an original, profound and vitally free art based on a refined and elegant simplicity. Some scholars have attributed these characteristics to art thus influenced by Zen: 1) asymmetry (freedom from form), 2) simplicity, 3) unpretentiousness (or wizened austerity), 4) naturalness (no-mind), 5) profundity, 6) transcendence (no hindrance) and 7) serenity (immovability). These characteristics are said to be inseparable and unified by spiritual enlightenment inherent in the training of the serene reflection practice. In my opinion, however, the characteristics of Zen art can be summed up by simplicity, profundity, creativity and vitality.

d. *What is Serene Reflection Meditation (Sōtō Zen)?*

In China the most popular of the Zen schools was the Lin-chi (Rinzai). However, in Japan the Ts'ao-Tung (J. Sōtō) School enjoys the greatest popularity. The Rinzai School in Japan mainly enjoyed the favor of the Shogunate and Daimyos (feudal lords) while, in contrast to this, the Sōtō School penetrated deeply into the hearts of the common people. In addition to Sōtō and Rinzai Schools in Japan, there is still another Zen School known as the Ōbaku School. This originally was affiliated with Rinzai, but since its founder in Japan, an immigrant Chinese priest named Ingen (1592–1673 C.E.), lived on Mt. Ōbaku in China, he called his school of Zen the Ōbaku School. Ingen introduced this school into Japan during the Tokugawa Period. Since the Meditation Schools of the Ming Dynasty had already attached great importance to *nembutsu* (invoking the name of a Buddha to attain salvation), this may be regarded as the distinctive feature of the Ōbaku School. In contemporary Japan, Rinzai counts 6,000 temples; Sōtō, 15,000 and Ōbaku, a mere 500. The three Meditation Schools combined have more than 8,000,000 followers and can boast of the second largest clergy of any Buddhist sect in Japan. The meditation which has been introduced to the West is largely Rinzai. Rinzai makes use

of the *kōan*, a classic dialogue between master and disciple
which at times may appear quite irrational or irrelevant, but
which ends in the enlightenment of the disciple. Enlightenment
is sought by meditation on the kōan. The Serene Reflection
School, although it is the largest of the meditation schools in
Japan and has penetrated deeply into the hearts of the people, is
little known abroad; however, there are increasing signs that it
will become better known in the West. Serene reflection claims
descent from Ch'ing-yuan Hsing-ssu (J. Seigen Gyōshi), a
disciple of the Sixth Ancestor Hui-neng (J. Daikan Enō). Tung-
shan Lian-chieh (J. Tōzan Ryōkai, 807–869 C.E.) who came
three generations after Ch'ing-yuan (J. Seigen Gyōshi), and his
disciple Ts'ao-shan Pen-chi (J. Sōzan Honjaku, 840–901 C.E.)
are considered founders of the Sōtō School in China.

   In the *Sayings of Tung-shan* (J. Tōzan Ryōkai) the origin
of the name of the school is explained as follows: "As the
profound style of Tung-shan made itself felt in all parts of the
Empire, masters of the school, in order to show their respect for
him, call the school the Tung-Ts'ao (Tōsō) school." T'ung-
Ts'ao (J. Tōsō) appears to have been the name by which the
Ts'ao-Tung (J. Sōtō) School was first known. Later the characters were reversed for euphonic reasons. This took place not too
long after the death of Ts'ao-shan (J. Sōzan), which probably
occurred about 915 C.E. According to another theory, however,
the name came from Ts'ao-chi Hui-neng (J. Sōkei Enō) and

Tung-shan Lian-chieh (J. Tōzan Ryōkai). However, this explanation is considered to be somewhat unlikely, being derived more from religious faith than veracity. Dōgen pays homage to Sōkei (J. Enō) and Tōzan, referring to them as "old" Buddhas. However, his treatment of Sōzan differs considerably. The present Sōtō School is not regarded as having descended from the line of Sōzan, but rather from Ungo Dōyō, a disciple of Tōzan. The name of the Sōtō School was popularized in Japan by Keizan (1269–1325 C.E.) who is two generations removed from Dōgen.

In China it was the Rinzai and Ummon Schools which enjoyed great popularity during the Sung Dynasty. At first, the Sōtō School did not make much headway, but as time passed, it gradually increased in strength. The Chinese Sōtō School did not put its main effort in the practice of the kōan exercise, but rather emphasized serene reflection meditation, the identity between understanding and training, the importance of continual religious training and the ideal of making the meditation come alive as a vital force within our everyday lives.

The kōan is a classic theme in the search for enlightenment by a pupil of Zen which serves as a guide for later generations. It is convenient insofar as it enables one to penetrate into the essence of meditation. However, when too much importance is attached to the kōan, there is a danger that one cannot see beyond the kōan, and it then becomes a hindrance to the fundamental religious spirit of "passing beyond and directly entering" (*itchō jikinyū*).

So, while the Serene Reflection School does not deny the usefulness of the kōan on one hand, it does not emphasize its unrestricted practice on the other. It sees training in everyday life itself as the religious experience (*kenshō* or *satori*) and as the real way for living within Buddhism. In serene reflection meditation, practice, enlightenment and wisdom are all fused into one. The Sixth Ancestor Hui-neng (J. Enō) succinctly summarized this by saying "meditation and wisdom are not two separate entities." This harmony between enlightenment and training is called in Japan *gyōge-sōō*, i.e., the reciprocity of training and enlightenment. Masters of the Sōtō School must be people who have deeply realized this reciprocity of training and enlightenment, the harmonization of words and actions, body and mind. No matter how trifling their words or actions may appear, we cannot neglect them for a moment, we must always pay the utmost respect to them. This attitude may be understood as a complete commitment to continual religious training *(gyōji memmitsu)* and devotion to applying the meditation to the details of ordinary life. In this, we can see the popular democratic aspect of the serene reflection tradition. The democratic spirit of the East appears especially in *samu* where Zen masters and trainees work together on equal terms.

e. The Religion of Great Masters Dōgen and Keizan

The age produces the great man; the great man produces the new age. Great Master Dōgen (1200–1253 C.E.) embarked on his journey to China at the age of 24 together with Myōzen (1163–1225 C.E.), the disciple of Eisai, to study Buddhism there.

In China, he visited various Buddhist masters, but finally he became a disciple of Ju-ching (J. Tendō Nyojō, 1163–1238 C.E.) on Mt. T'ien-t'ung (J. Tendō). He devoted himself wholeheartedly to his search for enlightenment, and after two years with the master, he attained complete freedom of mind and body (*shinjin datsuraku*), i.e., enlightenment. At last he was able to rid himself of the illusions of ego with which he had been so completely shackled, and he could now bask in the indescribable bliss of the Truth of Buddhism for the first time. And Dōgen, because of his deep understanding, continued his religious training as before. At the age of 28, four years after he had left Japan, following the wishes of his master Ju-ching he returned to Japan to propagate the Serene Reflection School there. For awhile after his return he made Kyōto, then the capital, the center of his activities and spent his time teaching and writing. Especially in the Kōshō-ji Temple at Uji did he teach the laity and the monks alike with a view to inspiring in them the spirit of Zen training. His stay in Kyōto covered more than ten years. During this time his practical achievements were great. Finally, he agreed to the supplications of Hatano Yoshishige and at the age of 44 moved to Echizen in the present Fukui Prefecture where he founded the Eihei-ji Temple. He continued his pious labors there for ten years until his death at the age of 53.

He transmitted the True Law to all sincere seekers who came to him, thus laying a solid foundation for the Serene Reflection Meditation School, accounting for its present day greatness. We can say briefly that the greatness of Dōgen is threefold: first, the depth of his thought; second, the total commitment to religious training as he saw it; and third, the loftiness of his character. His principal work is known as the *Shōbōgenzō,* literally The Eye and Treasury of the True Teaching, which consists of ninety-five chapters. It is written in the colloquial Japanese, not the classical Chinese which was so popular during Dōgen's day. It has a powerful style, at once concise and profound. Its sharp logic and deep theory place it in the forefront of Japanese philosophy which is sincerely trying to find some common ground between East and West. It is, therefore, not at all strange to hear a scholar not of the Sōtō School proclaim: "The essence of Japanese culture cannot be properly grasped without an understanding of the ideas of

Dōgen. We Japanese regard Dōgen's profound thought as an unending source of inspiration from which we are able to draw a large measure of self-confidence."

However, the greatness of Dōgen is not simply due to the excellence of his theories. Dōgen develops his ideas with a precise logic, based on direct experience of the Unborn, and at no time does he toy with intellectual speculations divorced from reality. Training and understanding are to Dōgen inseparably bound to each other. The strict regulations governing the life of the monastic trainees and priests laid down in his work, *Eihei Daishingi,* make this quite clear. Buddhism demands that we know ourselves thoroughly, experience deeply our own mind and body. To experience deeply is not merely a matter of knowing in an intellectual sense, but vitally feeling with our entire body as well as mind. By such training does the real life of the Buddha appear.

The greatness of Dōgen rests upon his lofty character in which a perfect harmony is achieved between deep theory and thorough-going practice. Dōgen cast aside worldly honors and rewards and eschewed the powerful and aristocratic families. He was content with the humble black robes of the priest, rejecting more elegant ones. He spent the last ten years of his life in the mountains of Echizen solely occupied with trying to train serious men no matter how few their number might be. He rejected a sizable gift from the then Regent Hojo Tokiyori because he felt that it had been given without sufficient reason. Likewise, he sent back to the Imperial Court purple robes which were offered him by the Imperial Family.

Dōgen consistently viewed Buddhism not from the narrow view of any school, but from Buddhism as a whole, steadfastly refusing to recognize such terms as Zen School or Sōtō School. He rejected the Heian-Kamakura period idea of *mappō* thought, i.e., that 1500 years after the death of the Buddha the world entered upon a thoroughly degenerate phase in which few, if any, people could attain to an understanding of the True Law. But many priests of the Heian and Kamakura periods accommodated their teachings to *mappō* thought, believing that few could actually find real understanding. Dōgen argued that man must strive even harder in his religious life just because it is the *mappō* period, and encouraged his followers to do so, because he *knew* it was possible to find the Truth.

Dōgen did not simply copy the idea of the meditation schools in China which used the meditation practice merely as a means to attain a religious experience. Bodhidharma, having duly received the attestation of enlightenment from his master, preached that man must come to a realization that he is possessed of the Buddha Nature from the outset. Following this to its natural conclusion, it becomes evident that since we possess the Buddha Nature, we are consequently in a state of enlightenment or may be considered Buddha in our own right.

In Buddhism we call such a realization "the original affirmation" (*honshō*). "It is heretical to believe that training and enlightenment are separate for, in Buddhism, the two are one and the same. Since training embraces enlightenment, the very beginning of training contains the whole of original enlightenment" [*Zen is Eternal Life*, "Bendowa," 1999, p. 186], i.e., the affirmation that we are enlightened from the outset. Therefore, we may regard serene reflection meditation as a practice which is identical with being Buddha and not simply a means to reach the stage of Buddhahood. Enlightenment is found in religious observance, and religious observances in enlightenment. The two are known as *honshō myōshū*, i.e., original enlightenment is simultaneously wondrous training. The practice mentioned here is unending; therefore, although one realizes enlightenment, one continues religious training as before. Even if one should become Buddha, no interruption in religious endeavors may take place. If enlightenment is to be considered only as a goal, then meditation can be regarded as nothing more than a means to reach that goal. This would indicate that once the goal is reached, the means will be cast aside. But to Dōgen meditation is not merely a means to an end, it is the end itself. This attitude toward meditation, which we call *shikan taza* or "wholehearted Zazen," transcends the distinction between religious striving and enlightenment itself. When one is firmly in a state of enlightenment, everyday life itself becomes a religious exercise in expressing our gratitude to the

Buddha. Dōgen remarks about this: "The life of this one day, to-day, is absolutely vital life; your body is deeply significant....This Buddha Nature is itself the Buddha and, should you awaken to a complete understanding thereof, your gratitude to the Buddhas will know no bounds." Every moment of each day is absolutely vital life and is sacred unto itself for this reason and cannot come again. In Bhadderaratta Sūtta there is this passage: "Do with all your heart what you must do today. Who can know the death of tomorrow?" The essence of Buddhism and the religious striving to express our gratitude consist then in living every day in Truth.

Two generations after Dōgen, during the time of Keizan (1268–1325 C.E.), the Serene Reflection School made a great step forward in strengthening its social basis and laid the foundation for building a steady religious order. While Dōgen and Keizan differed in some elements of the teaching, their basic viewpoint and belief were the same. Keizan especially stressed selflessness in action for the benefit of all beings.

f. What is the Role of Sōtō Zen Practice?

_____

1) Since its introduction in Japan the world view of life which Sōtō Zen teaches has served as a spiritual cornerstone. This is because serene reflection meditation or silent prayer is the basic structure for all religious exercise. It makes religious training of both mind and body vital and essential, rejecting the illusion which mistakes the side path for the main road.

2) The practice of meditation breaks through the impasse of present day cultural weaknesses and provides a powerful reinforcement for true culture, based on the cultivation of the human spirit. Because of its inherent profundity, simplicity and vital freedom, it can enable present day culture to cast aside its unessential complexity which has resulted in the inability to know the Unborn.

3) In our present life which has become so mechanized and is filled with anxiety, Zen provides time for quiet contemplation and introspection which can greatly enrich our lives and assume great significance for us.

4) In the communal living conditions of monasteries, upper and lower classes are equalized and work is carried on in such a manner as to make life very democratic. Trainees meditate, eat and sleep in the same room according to the Zen

tradition, and this kind of living not only produces a feeling of deep friendship, but also a sense of collective responsibility gradually develops.

5) The serene reflection practice does not go to the extreme of materialism or idealism. It firmly holds that mind and matter are inseparable. Avoiding the extreme viewpoint of either materialism or idealism, Zen finds a middle path. Mind and matter are but two sides of reality, and to attempt to separate them and cling to either leads to dualism which Buddhism rejects.

6) The meditation practice adapts itself to the individuality and capacity of each person. It is, therefore, able to guide one correctly to a deep understanding of one's Real Nature. It is capable of producing disciples who receive the Transmission from a true master and who can exceed their masters. A true master reveals his individuality and brings it to bear as a vital force not only in the period in which he lives but also in succeeding ages.

7) The practice of serene reflection meditation has penetrated deeply into the lives of the common people where it has nourished the spirit which holds the way to enlightenment for ordinary people. This is because Buddhism is not God's religion, but a human religion, not a religion for heaven, but one for the earth. The Serene Reflection School remained aloof

from the great powers in Japan such as *shoguns* and *daimyos* and always maintained close contact with the common people, holding steadfastly to the spirit that life itself is Zen.

8) Buddhist meditation, which aims at acquiring nothing, kept itself pure and did not fall into the pitfalls of superstition which aims at receiving material benefits in this world through religious practice. We believe that superstition and science are incompatible. Sōtō Zen is a pure religion which is rooted in the correct Buddha Dharma.

9) A philosophical foundation for modern thought and faith is considered an absolute necessity. We believe that the thought of Great Master Dōgen can give important suggestions and stimuli to the task of synthesizing the philosophy of both the East and the West. In particular, one chapter of *Shōbōgenzō* called "*Uji*," which contains Dōgen's theory of time, has much to offer Western philosophy.

10) As long as mankind possesses an inherent spirituality, both men and women are equal insofar as their spiritual capacities are concerned. Great Master Dōgen taught from a lofty viewpoint the equality of men and women long before the Renaissance and emphasized the dignity of the human character. This is a powerful stimulus to democratic Japan. [It is important for all nations of the world to open the doors of spiritual equality to all persons. Editor's note.]

11) Buddhism is a religion of peace and has never brought about a war. When we understand its doctrine of Dependent Origination (J. *engi* Skt. *patīccasamuppāda*) i.e., the karmic cause of suffering and its refusal to admit the existence of an indestructible soul or ego, we naturally turn toward peace. Then will mankind enjoy happiness. Sōtō Zen, which received the support of the common people, always avoided any form of bloodshed and guided the people into the path of culture and peace.

12) Toynbee emphasizes that the creative minority has to undergo a two-sided process of withdrawal and return. The former means basically looking inward and finding one's True Self; the latter refers to re-entering society and working for others. C. G. Jung, the Swiss psychotherapist, puts stress on the former in his individuation process. Sociologist Pitirim Sorokin, on the other hand, has focused on creative altruism in social activity. Toynbee has a good intellectual understanding of withdrawal and return; however, Dōgen emphasized their unity. This is made clear in his synthesizing of enlightenment and training: "original enlightenment and wondrous training." This is Dōgen's great contribution—training embraces enlightenment and enlightenment embraces training. In other words, all of original enlightenment comes with training and all of wondrous training comes with enlightenment. They are in fact

one. [Out of training and enlightenment one can realize the Eternal and use that understanding for the benefit of all living things. Editor's note.]

Buddhist meditation practice now has spread across the seas and is exciting interest in the West. This unique thought and culture is urging Westerners on to open a new field of endeavor. We have taken this occasion to make clear some of the principles of Buddhist meditation, particularly of the Serene Reflection School, which we feel will contribute to a deeper understanding and through that to world peace and the happiness of mankind. In conclusion, we should like to add that we expect that the future of the Serene Reflection School which is at once cultural, peaceful and constructive will have much to contribute to the world. Particularly do we feel that the thought and faith of Great Master Dōgen follow the ideals held by all humanity and possess a broad objectivity which is universally applicable.

We should like to end this article with the fervent hope that henceforth thinkers throughout the world will find deep interest in the field of serene reflection Buddhist meditation and will undertake seriously its study and practice.

APPENDIX II

CORRESPONDENCE

The following documents are part of a series of letters between Kohō Zenji and Miss Peggy Kennett which show that she was asked by him to come to Japan and study at the temple Sōji-ji, one of the two Headquarter Temples where Sōtō Zen monks train to become full priests and where Kohō Zenji was the Abbot. Although no woman and person who had been born in a foreign country had been, officially, at Sōji-ji in living memory, Kohō Zenji had long championed the cause of women's education and was now extending it to someone he felt was worthy to be his Dharma Heir. It was not necessarily a popular decision at that time in Japan. Rev. Jiyu-Kennett's presence in the monastery created considerable controversy including accusations that she had never been asked to come. These documents are published here as part of the historic record. Rumors and accusations, although contrary to the Buddhist Precepts, are present in all cases where controversial decisions are taken. During his lifetime, the Buddha had instances in which people accused him of wrongdoing to discredit him, and his life was threatened by those jealous of his success. There is no reason to think that complaints would not arise when leading monks make controversial decisions in the Twentieth Century. Those of us in the West who have benefited from hearing the Buddhist teachings as a result of Kohō Zenji's courage to transmit the Truth to Rev. Jiyu-Kennett are profoundly grateful. His decision has touched the lives of thousands of people who might not otherwise have been able to hear these teachings.

This first document is a letter from Kohō Zenji to Miss Peggy Kennett from early in 1961 inviting her to come to "join his monastery."

Kennet

create thanks for your hearty teen for me. Now we recieved it on my bed in hospital. But dont worry of my health. It is so slight ill. After 5 day's I will leave my bed and he return my Temple. I'm so glad to met you in London. and Jack and you also nice Buddhist and with your hospitality to Buddha. And I'm also hoping to come our country for what to see me and be join my monastry if you can be able do so.

Please sometimes give me your letter yesterday Jack Austin gave his letter. In it I found he accepted his orditional document in Soto Zen. I'm so glad to read it and had sent him my greate congraturation. Say good regard for him. And please keep you well. Good-bye.

Sincerely yours.

Chisan Kohō.

19th 1961

The second document is a letter in which she is asking him to send a formal letter that she could take to the embassy to get a visa.

Venerable Sir,

I am deeply sorry to hear that you spent so long in hospital and hope that you are now fully recovered. I am also deeply sorry to have kept you waiting so long for a reply to your letter but I had hoped to send some photographs of the children's Sōtō Zen class here in London. Unfortunately they were not very successful and have to be retaken. Please accept my apologies. I will send them as soon as they are available.

I feel deeply honoured by your acceptance of me at your temple and also of your kindness in allowing me to teach in one of your schools as I said in my last letter I hope eventually to return to England to start a Sōtō Zen Temple here. The

Japanese Embassy here in London have asked me
to request you to send them a formal letter

stating that you have invited me to teach and
study at your Temple and also to state how
long you estimate my stay will last   I am
sorry to have to ask you to do this but they
will not issue me a visa until they receive
a letter from you. (I shall not, in any case,
be able to travel for some months since I have
to save the money for the fare.)

    I have delivered your messages to Mr. Austin and
Mr. Humphreys and they both thank you. Mr. Austin
sends his regards.

    Can you recommend anything for me to study
here in England that ~~that~~ will help me on arrival

at your monastery?.   There is nothing available here
on Soto except the book I use for the childer ~ which
was sent to me by the Rev. Ernest Hunt.

I am so looking forward to coming,

Yours obediently,

Peggy T. N. Kennett,

Dear Peggy,
I'm pleased to tell you that I
could manage to translate what
you wrote

As I think it better you post
the letter by your hand, I enclose it
herewith

At the foot-note I mentioned how
hard you are trying to make fund
without help of Buddhist society. I hope
he would understand.

T. Nadagami

The third document is the Japanese original of the letter of guarantee which Kohō Zenji gave on a yearly basis until his death. (This document is item B referred to on page 149.) The guarantees were also extended after his death until Rev. Kennett came to the United States in November of 1969.

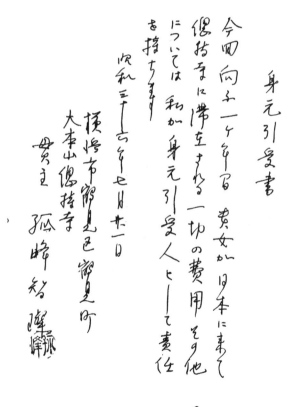

The fourth document is a translation of the document of guarantee.

> *For the coming period of a year, as your guarantor I will take responsibility for all your expenses and other needs while you are staying in Japan at Sōji-ji.*

> *July 1, 1961.*
> *Yokohama City, Tsurumi-ku, Tsurumi-chō*
> *Daihonzan Sōji-ji*

> *Kohō Chisan, Abbot*
> */signed in Japanese and sealed /*

> *Chisan Kohō*
> */signed in English /*

The fifth document is an edited version of a letter in English which includes a translation of Kohō Zenji's letter of invitation to Miss Kennett and the accompanying letter of guarantee for her care during her first year of training at Sōji-ji. The original of the translation was rather badly marked up in the process of translating it from Japanese and this transcription has been done to facilitate it being read. The translator may not have been too fluent in English, but the information is clear:

Dear Peggy,
I am so pleased to have letters in reply to yours, which I sent the other day, enclosed with a guarantee for your stay in Japan for one year.

A paper that I marked B is the guarantee you want. It is stated that the Abbot will take all responsibility as a guarantor for any expenses and other things you require to stay in the Sōji Temple for one year to come, signed in his name and dated 21st July 1961.

Another one marked A is his letter to you dated 21st July in the morning of the day, which gist is as follows:
"Thank you for your letter of 7th July. I am pleased to hear that you are keeping well off and you are endeavouring to make good progress of your study of Buddhism since last winter.

Would you please come and study in my temple regarding Zen. I recommend you to practice your study by staying in my temple together with priests at least for one year.

As I would commend myself to be guarantor for all expenses of your living here during your stay, I hope you come any time as you wish after you receive this letter.

Although it is rather hot now in Japan it seems to me a good chance you come and practice while you get aspiration for it, and study for about one year without worrying anything else during stay.

I shall be pleased to help you for everything you may require for procedure with Japanese Embassy.

Give my best regard to Mr. Austin.

Yours truly,"
Chisan Kohō /signed/

That's all.
Congratulations!

Enclosed please find both letters marked A and B and go ahead for visa showing them to staff of the Embassy.

/signed by the translator/

Document 6 is the translation of the certificate accompanying the presentation of Kohō Zenji's ashes to Shasta Abbey. It is included within the "Important Announcement" article written by Rev. Rōshi Jiyu-Kennett, O.B.C., Abbess, and published in *The Journal of Shasta Abbey*, October-November-December 1984. The original of the certificate is not included here, but it did appear when this article was published in *The Journal of Shasta Abbey*.

IMPORTANT ANNOUNCEMENT
Rev. Rōshi Jiyu-Kennett, O.B.C., Abbess

On the 2nd. of November, Rev. Ekō Little and Rev. Kinsei Tower went to the Far East for the purpose of attending a symposium on the future of Sōtō Zen temples in the West of which Shasta Abbey is one. Whilst I will leave it to Rev. Little to inform the readership at a later date of the actual decisions reached during the symposium, there were several other events which, at least form the point of view of Shasta Abbey, are of far greater importance.

After the death of Rev. Seck Kim Seng, Archbishop of Malacca, Malaysia, Shasta Abbey received his ashes for interment here in the shrine of the ancestors, known in Shasta Abbey as the Kohō Zenji Shrine. As all of you know, Rev. Seck

Kim Seng was the Rinzai master who ordained me in Malacca in January of 1962. He supported me financially to a very large extent whilst I was studying in Japan as well as paying a considerable amount of my hospital expenses when I was taken seriously ill in 1967: Shasta Abbey was also the main beneficiary of his will. During the symposium in Japan, Rev. Little gave a slide presentation of the daily activities of Shasta Abbey in which was seen the enthronement of Rev. Seck Kim Seng's ashes. Rev. Little pointed out that, although the shrine was named for Rev. Keidō Chisan Kohō Zenji, there were none of his ashes to be found in the shrine. After the presentation was over, Rev. Korimatsu approached Rev. Little and pointed out that he felt certain that some of Rev. Kohō Zenji's ashes could be obtained for Shasta Abbey's shrine. The day after the symposium ended, Rev. Little and Rev. Tower visited Sōji-ji and spent a very happy afternoon with Rev. Umeda Zenji and his senior staff together with some of the officials of the Head Office. Rev. Umeda Zenji's chief jiisha, an old friend of mine named Rev. Okabe, on hearing about Shasta Abbey's lack of Rev. Kohō Zenji's ashes immediately made some telephone calls the results of which were that Rev. Little and Rev. Tower were invited to Fukujuin Temple, where my nephew in the Dharma, Rev. Kōryū Noguchi, presented them with some of Rev. Zenji's ashes and a certificate of authenticity. The certificate reads as follows:–

OFFICIAL DOCUMENT FOR *the reception of one part of the Venerable Ashes of Keidō Chisan Daishō (Great Priest Keidō Chisan) who passed away (crossed over) in function on November 1st. 1967, and was by Imperial Decree (given the title of) Enō Shidō Zenji (i.e. Abbot and Zen Master with complete fulfillment of attaining the Way) of Dai Hon Zan Sōji-ji, and Dokuju (Chief Priest) in the 18th. generation (these are) offered (provided) in a receptacle on November 14th. 1984, by the hands of Okabe Tokuyu Rōshi of Dōryō-ji Temple of Tōkyō, and entrusted to Rōshi Jiyu-Kennett of the United States of America as acknowledgement of being a Great Wisdom Rōshi in the 515th generation of the Buddhist era.*

(Tōkyō) Asakusa—Hashiba (place)

Fukujuin (temple)

Chikai Kōryū—(name of Rōshi)

(seal: Chikai Kōryū Fukujuin)

Needless to say, both I and the community of Shasta Abbey are overjoyed to receive this wonderful gift. We have temporarily enshrined the ashes and hope to hold a public ceremony for their viewing, reverencing and enshrinement some time early next year. In the meantime we want to express our heartfelt thanks to those who made it possible for us to receive this wonderful gift for our Founder's Hall and to thank my many relatives in the Dharma who have made it possible.

Rev. Little and Rev. Tower went to the graveyard of Sōji-
ji where they paid their respects to Rev. Kohō Zenji's stupa and
performed a memorial ceremony for him in my name and in
that of all of you. They were again assisted in this by Rev.
Okabe and several others of Umeda Zenji's staff. I would like
very much to thank the Sōji-ji authorities for their wonderful
assistance in these matters. The photograph shows Rev. Little
officially receiving the ashes from Rev. Noguchi at Fukujuin.

Note: While the portion of ashes received are enshrined in Shasta
Abbey's Founders Shrine, some of them were also sent to
Throssel Hole Buddhist Abbey in England by Rev. Jiyu-Kennett.

ABOUT THE AUTHOR

Rev. Keidō Chisan Kohō Zenji was born on August 16, 1879 in Toyama Prefecture, Japan. He was ordained as a Buddhist trainee by Kohō Hakugan of Eikō-ji Temple, Ishikawa Prefecture in 1892, and received the Dharma Transmission from Kohō Hakugan in 1901. He graduated from the Sōtō Zen Sect's (Kamazawa) University and entered Sōji-ji Temple in 1904. The next year he became the Abbot of Senpuku-ji Temple in Chiba Prefecture, and in 1907 he became the Abbot of the Raigaku-ji Temple in Nagano Prefecture.

In 1915 he became the Vice-Principal of the Sōtō Zen Church First Middle School. In 1918 he became the Principal of the Setagaya Middle School. He became the Treasurer of the Sōtō Zen Headquarters (Sōtōshu Shumucho) in 1926. In the following year he advanced to become the Abbot of Eikō-ji Temple and the Vice-Director of Daihonzan Sōji-ji. In 1937 he was promoted to be Director of Sōji-ji. In 1947 he received the post of Abbot of Saijō-ji Temple, which was quickly followed by promotion to Chief Abbot of Daihonzan Sōji-ji and Archbishop of the Kantō Plains, and receipt of the honor and the title Daikyōsei (Great Teacher) from the Emperor of Japan in 1948. During the next 12 years he made two tours of the West. Rev. P.T.N.H. Jiyu-Kennett

became his personal disciple in 1962, after he invited her to come
to Japan to study with him. She received the Dharma Transmission from him on May 28, 1963 and later received a Sei degree
(roughly equivalent to a Doctor of Divinity) from Daihonzan Sōji-
ji. While he was still Abbot of Sōji-ji, Kohō Zenji died on November 1, 1967 which is traditionally 'founder's day' in Zen Temples.
(It is a day to give thanks for the kindness of the Buddhas and
Ancestors who have dedicated their lives to the teaching and
transmitting of the Buddha's Truth.) In November of 1970 Rev.
Jiyu-Kennett established a training monastery and seminary in
Mt. Shasta, California in Kohō Zenji's name. He is the first
founder of Shasta Zan Chisan-ji (Shasta Abbey). In 1972 she
established a British monastery, Throssel Hole Buddhist Abbey,
where the Dharma transmitted to her from Kohō Zenji is flourishing in Great Britain and throughout Europe. In 1985 a portion of
his ashes were brought from Japan and were formally installed
in the Founder's Shrines at Shasta Abbey and Throssel Hole
Buddhist Abbey.

ABOUT THE ORDER OF
BUDDHIST CONTEMPLATIVES

The Order of Buddhist Contemplatives is a religious order practicing Serene Reflection Meditation (J. Sōtō Zen) as transmitted from the Very Reverend Keidō Chisan Kohō Zenji, Abbot of Daihonzan Sōji-ji in Yokohama Japan, to Reverend Master P.T.N.H. Jiyu-Kennett. Rev. Master Jiyu-Kennett came to the United States in 1969 and established Shasta Abbey in 1970. She founded the Order of Buddhist Contemplatives in 1978, serving as Head of the Order until her death in 1996. In North America, the Order now has Priories (congregational temples) in Albany and Maricopa, California; Eugene and Portland, Oregon; McKenna and Seattle, Washington; and Edmonton, Alberta and Vancouver, B.C., Canada. In Europe, Throssel Hole Buddhist Abbey in northern England was founded in 1972, and O.B.C. Priories are located in Edinburgh, Scotland, and Reading and Telford, England. There are also meditation groups affiliated with the Order in Great Britain, Canada, the United States, the Netherlands, and Germany. The Order has male and female monks; women and men have equal status and recognition and train together in the Buddhist priesthood; they are referred to as both monks and priests. The monastic order is celibate and vegetarian. In addition to monastics, the Order includes lay ministers throughout the world. The Head of the Order is Rev. Master Daizui MacPhillamy; its international headquarters are at Shasta Abbey. The Order publishes *The Journal of the Order of Buddhist Contemplatives* quarterly.

ABOUT THE MONASTERIES
OF THE ORDER

Shasta Abbey, located on sixteen forested acres near Mount Shasta city in northern California, is a seminary for the Buddhist priesthood and training monastery for both lay and monastic Buddhists and visitors. It was established in 1970 by Rev. Master P.T.N.H. Jiyu-Kennett, who was Abbess and spiritual director until her death in 1996. Buddhist training at Shasta Abbey is based on the practice of Serene Reflection Meditation and the keeping of the Buddhist Precepts. The monastery is home to over 30 ordained male and female monks and its Abbot is Rev. Master Ekō Little, a senior disciple of Rev. Master Jiyu-Kennett.

Guests and visitors follow a schedule that is similar to that of the monastic community, providing a balance of sitting meditation, work, ceremonial, and instruction in Buddhism. The schedule allows the mind of meditation to be cultivated and maintained throughout all aspects of daily life. Retreat guests stay at the Abbey's guest house, which accommodates about 40 people. All meals are vegetarian and are prepared in the Abbey kitchen. A stay at Shasta Abbey allows visitors to set aside their usual daily concerns, so that they may participate wholeheartedly in the spiritual life of the monastery.

In addition to its monastic and lay training programs, Shasta Abbey offers a Buddhist Supply service and publishes books through Shasta Abbey Press. For more information, call or write Shasta Abbey, 3724 Summit Drive, Mt. Shasta, California, 96067-9102; phone (530) 926-4208; fax (530) 926-0428; e-mail: shastaabbey@obcon.org.

Throssel Hole Buddhist Abbey is situated in a quiet valley in the north of England. It was founded in 1972 by Rev. Master Jiyu-Kennett as Throssel Hole Priory, and over the years has become a monastery and seminary for training priests of the Order, as well as a retreat and training center for a large European congregation. Its Abbot is Rev. Master Daishin Morgan, a senior disciple of the late Rev. Kennett.

The Abbey offers for lay guests a full and varied program, to which all are warmly invited. Experienced senior priests teach both meditation and how to use the Buddhist Precepts in establishing a daily practice. Through these means one can find the Truth, or Buddha Nature, at the heart of oneself and all beings. Training shows how to let go of the clinging that causes suffering, thus allowing this inner compassion and wisdom to enrich our lives. Guests meditate in the bright and spacious ceremony hall, and sleep there at night, dormitory-style, with complete privacy between men and women maintained. A large dining hall includes a small library and common room area for guests. By following the monastery's daily schedule, guests experience how it is that all activities of life—working, relaxing, reading, eating and sleeping—have true spiritual depth and value. For more information, call or write Throssel Hole Buddhist Abbey, Carrshield, nr. Hexham, Northumberland NE47 8AL, United Kingdom; phone +44 (0) 1434 345204 or fax +44 (0) 1434 345216.

ABOUT PINE MOUNTAIN BUDDHIST TEMPLE

Pine Mountain Buddhist Temple and Meditation Retreat is a temple of the Order of Buddhist Contemplatives. It was founded in the name of Rev. Master Jiyu-Kennett in 1979 as the Santa Barbara Zen Priory; its name has been changed and the Temple has moved to 941 Lockwood Valley Road, Maricopa, California 93252. The editor of this book, Rev. Jishō Perry, is co-Prior with Rev. Phoebe van Woerden. The Temple is a training center and monastic residence with a regular schedule of meditation instruction, daily meditation and services, Buddhist Festivals, retreats and Dharma talks on Buddhist practice. The Temple is located in the National Forest 40 miles north of Ojai on 20 acres of land surrounded by the California Coast Range Mountains. Monks from the Temple also visit meditation groups in Oak View, Santa Barbara and Morro Bay–Los Osos. The Temple can be reached by calling (661) 322-9016, extension 08103, or by leaving a message at (805) 905-3550.

O.B.C. Website: www.obcon.org